Contents

INTRODUCTION

You probably know a few things about the *Titanic*, but what do you really know?

You've probably read a little about the Titanic in a history class and I bet you've probably seen that movie with Leonard DiCaprio. Sure you may have been made to watch it or maybe you slept through it. But the point is that you already know a little bit about the Titanic.

But the reality is that most of what you know about the Titanic probably concerns the actual disaster.

Unfortunately, that is only part of the story. There is much much more to learn about with several questions that will be raised.

For instance, "how long did it take to build the ship?"

"How many people were involved in the construction?"

In this book, we will also explore such things as what the passengers ate before the disaster and will cover some strange connections the Titanic had with another doomed ship.

All of these questions and more are answered in the following book in a lively manner that will at times put you on the deck with the first-class passengers! This book will bring the Titanic back to life in a way that few other histories of Titanic have done.

Although this book follows a general chronology of the Titanic's life, it focuses on themes and topics that are not only historically important, but also interesting for you the reader in the twenty-first century. Yes, the Titanic sank just over 100 years ago but its cultural impact continues to be felt today around the world in many ways, especially in film and other fictional accounts.

Ultimately the point of this book is to educate you the reader about the Titanic in a way that is entertaining and fun.

It's broken up into six easy chapters, each with fifteen stories about the chapter's main topic. They'll introduce you to the most important events and people relating to the Titanic's construction and ultimate sinking in an interesting way. They'll also help you understand the facts in a way that will allow you to discuss them at your next dinner party or history class. Each chapter also comes with a whole section full of quick, surprising facts to wow your friends and a few challenging trivia questions to test your knowledge.

Some of the things you learn in this book will be interesting, perplexing, and even bizarre, but they are all true.

So get ready to answer these intriguing questions…

How did the idea of trans-Atlantic steamships come about?

Where was the Titanic built?

How many pets were on the Titanic?

Why were some people heroes while others were zeroes during the disaster?

And much, much more!

CHAPTER ONE
THE GOLDEN ERA OF OCEAN LINERS

The story of the RMS *Titanic* began years before its maiden and tragic, final voyage across the icy waters of the north Atlantic Ocean. The Titanic was actually at the tail end of an era when passenger steamships carried passengers, mail, and other goods across both the Atlantic and Pacific Oceans.

The golden era of ocean liners was powered by two major occurrences that were changing the world in the nineteenth century: the Industrial Revolution and immigration from primarily Europe and to some extent Asia, to the United States. The invention of steam power lead to the creation of steam ships, which were much sturdier, bigger, and faster than their wind powered sloop predecessors. Almost immediately after they were invented, steam powered passenger ships could traverse the Atlantic in the span of two or three weeks instead of two or three months.

This ship's crew just had to make sure there was enough coal or something else to burn to keep the engine going.

Immigration and colonization always helped spur the golden age of the ocean liners.

Millions of immigrants from Ireland, the British Isles, Scandinavia, and the German speaking kingdoms made their way across the Atlantic Ocean during the nineteenth and early twentieth centuries on ocean liners. Oftentimes, as was the case on the Titanic, immigrants were cramped together in third class cabins well more well to do passengers enjoyed the amenities of first-class. Ocean liners also took passengers to and from Britain's many colonies around the world.

There is a good chance that if you are an American reading this, one of your ancestors first came to America on board one of these type of ships.

Thankfully for you it wasn't the Titanic!

Robert Fulton Gets It Started

In order to understand the background of the Titanic we have to look at history of ocean liners and you can't do that without talking about Robert Fulton (1765-1815). Fulton was an American inventor and a product of the Enlightenment and the Industrial Age and a man who would change the world with his inventions.

Fulton was a precocious young lad who showed a talent for science and engineering at a young age. When he turned twenty, Fulton moved to Europe where he witnessed and benefited from the Industrial Revolution first hand. The young Fulton was able to observe early steam engines, which gave him the idea to use them to power ships.

Now it should be pointed out that the first steam powered boats and ships began sailing on the shores and rivers of Europe in the late eighteenth century, but they were few and far between.

And they were usually government enterprises, which meant they were off limits to the public.

In true American spirit, Fulton decided that he would build the first commercial steamship. When Fulton returned to the United States in 1806, he and his partner Robert Livingston built the first commercial steamship, named the *North River Steamboat* (later renamed the *Clermont*). Fulton and Livingston offered passengers a round trip excursion from New York City to Albany, New York on the Hudson River. The approximately 300 mile round trip journey took about sixty hours, which is incredibly long time by today's standards, but not in 1807.

Not only that, the passengers found the trip extremely relaxing and enjoyable!

Fulton soon expanded his operations and others would follow, competing to be the first offer trans-Atlantic passenger steamship service.

The era of the ocean liner was officially born!

Crossing the Atlantic

Although Robert Fulton may have led the way in terms of the idea of passenger steam liners, going up and down rivers was far different than crossing the ocean. For the first few decades, steamboats were primarily used on rivers. Entrepreneurs quickly followed Fulton's lead by building steamboats for the Mississippi, Ohio, and Missouri rivers, but technology and people's nerves needed to catch up before trans-Atlantic travel would become a regular occurrence.

Steamboats were big and needed lots of coal to power their engines.

And if they ran out of coal in the middle of the Atlantic they had to rely on sails to pick out the slack!

In 1818, the passenger ship *Savanah* left Savanah, Georgia and arrived in Liverpool, England twenty-seven days later. The Savanah was the first ship to use the SS title (steamship), although she was a hybrid. The Savanah was primarily powered by sails, but also had a ninety horse power steam engine that powered two sixteen feet paddlewheels.

Paddlewheel-sail hybrid ships followed the Savanah through the 1830s until the propeller replaced the impractical paddlewheel in the 1840s. By the 1850s, most ocean liners were using steam power exclusively with a screw propeller and iron hulls replaced wooden hulls.

By the mid-nineteenth century ocean liners were making regular trans-Atlantic voyages and by the late nineteenth century most of the world could be reached by steamship. The creation of ocean liners was truly a technological leap for humanity, but it was not without its problems.

Early Maritime Disasters

When you consider the fact that millions of people traveled on steam powered ocean liners from the mid-1800s until the mid-1900s and only a few thousand died in ship wrecks and other disasters, then it can be considered one of the safest modes of travel in human history.

This was especially true if the passenger liner companies took the appropriate safety precautions.

Hundreds of ocean liners ran into problems, but because their owners had enough lifeboats and their crews were competent, casualties were kept to a minimum.

The reality is, though, that ocean liner travel was a new concept in the nineteenth century and it used new technologies, so mistakes and disasters were bound to happen. Perhaps the owners and crew of the Titanic could have studied some of these disasters. Or maybe they did but disaster struck the Titanic too suddenly.

In any event, here are a few of the most important pre-Titanic ocean liner disasters.

The SS *Austria* was a German owned, Scottish built ocean liner steamship that was first launched in June 1857. On September 1, 1858 the Austria left Hamburg, Germany on her third voyage to the United States with 542 passengers, many of them immigrants. Many of the immigrants were crammed into the steerage or lower deck of the ship, which in the early days of the ocean liners served as the quarters for the poorest of the immigrant travelers. It was not uncommon for disease and illness to break out in the steerage decks, so the ships' crews would often fumigate these sections using methods that today would be considered unethical and certainly unsafe.

On September 13, as the ship was in the middle of the Atlantic, the crew of the Austria decided to fumigate the steerage section by dipping a hot chain into a bucket of tar, but the chain fell, causing a fire that quickly enveloped the entire ship.

Most of the ship was overcome with the smoke and those who didn't succumb to the smoke were engulfed in flames.

Only eight-nine of the Austria's 542 passengers survived.

The next major maritime disaster to happen was the sinking of the RMS *Atlantic* in 1873. The Atlantic was a 600 horsepower steamship with four masts for sail and was owned by the White Star Line, which also happened to be the Titanic's company.

But we'll get to the White Star Line a little later.

On April 1, 1873, as the Atlantic was nearing New York as it had numerous times before, it ran into rocks near Nova Scotia, Canada and sank, killing 535 of the 952 on board. The sinking of the Atlantic was the worst maritime disaster in history.

That was until 1898 when the French ocean liner *La Bourgogne* sank.

The La Bourgogne was an extremely fast ocean liner for the period, traveling at seventeen knots (twenty miles per hour), it set a record in 1886 for the fastest trans-Atlantic voyage by a mail carrier.

But all the speed in the world couldn't save the La Bourgogne on July 4, 1898 when it collided with another ship in heavy fog off Sable Island, Canada.

La Bourgogne was carrying 506 passengers and 220 crew, but only 173 survived. Of the survivors, though, only seventy were passengers. Although the officers did in fact go down with the ship and only the purser survived, many of the non-officers survived and some were said to have abandoned their posts.

With 549 fatalities, the sinking of the La Bourgogne surpassed the Atlantic as the worst maritime disaster in history.

A World Wide Web

Today, we can connect with anyone or any idea in the world via the Internet almost instantaneously, but the era of the ocean liners was the first true period of an interconnected world. True, the connections took weeks instead of seconds, but it was the first time in history where you could get to just about anywhere in the world if you had a minimum amount of money and the time.

Of course, there was a good chance you'd be relegated to the steerage section, but even in the cramped and sometimes disease ridden bowels of the ship you were guaranteed a ride from point A to point B.

Since most of the major ocean liner companies were based in Europe and Europe was still the center of the world's power structure at the time, most of the major ports were in European cities, especially in England. Liverpool, Southampton, and Bristol were three of the busiest ports in England, while the Irish city of Queenstown (now Cobh), was also bustling on any given day with travelers.

The French harbors of Le Havre and Cherbourg saw quite a bit of ocean liner traffic, as did Hamburg and Bremerhaven in Germany.

From those cities the ocean liners made their most common voyages across the Atlantic to New York City, bringing a combination of mail, tourists, and immigrants in search of the American dream.

Smaller ports in the Mediterranean Sea for often the staging point for immigrants bound for the United States. Just as with the other routes, Mediterranean ships carried a combination of pleasure cruisers and immigrants, but would usually stop in France or England where the immigrants would then transfer to other ships before continuing on to America.

The South Atlantic was also served by many of the major ocean liner companies. Waves of immigrants were brought to Buenos Aries, Argentina and British colonists and officials were brought back and forth from Africa.

Almost as busy as the North Atlantic routes were the Far East routes, which covered a much larger part of the world. Routes between Britain and Australia became well-established and frequently used by the late nineteenth century and ocean liners laden with Chinese immigrants in the steerage section routinely brought passengers from ports in Hong Kong and Shanghai to San Francisco.

By 1910, the ocean liner companies had truly created the first world wide web with their routes that served most major coastal cities in the world.

Sure, it is a far cry from the internet, but everything has to have a start, right?

Royal Mail Ships

So we learned that SS stands for steamship, but what about RMS? RMS was an acronym for "Royal Mail Ship" or Royal Mail Steamer.

Now that that is cleared up, you are probably wondering what the royal mail has to do with ocean liner or the Titanic. The answer is quite simple: the British government contracted many of the major ocean liners to deliver mail across the ocean.

Remember, the era of the ocean liners began decades before the first flight and even when the Titanic sank, it would still be nearly twenty years until Charles Lindbergh made his flight across the Atlantic.

The RMS designation first began in 1840 for British government ships to deliver the mail and was expanded in 1850 to include private liners that were awarded government contracts.

During World War I and World War II, RMS ships often became unintended targets of German U-Boats. Although the Germans generally tried to avoid torpedoing passenger ships, accidents happened, as was the case with the *Lusitania*.

When the Titanic left on its ill-fated journey across the Atlantic, it was laden with plenty of letters written by people inquiring about their loved ones in the New World.

Four Funnel Liners

If you had to give a physical description of the Titanic based on what you know from seeing pictures of it in book and documentaries, or recreations of it in the movies, you would no doubt describe it as being big.

But probably more importantly you would describe its four large smoke stacks or funnels.

Four funnel ocean liners were the result of both a need due to the increased size of ships in the era and also due to public perceptions. As shipping companies built larger ships to hold more passengers, more boilers were needed to power the ships and bigger stacks were needed for the steam to escape. Cosmetically speaking, the large stacks began to be seen as symbols of a ship's power and ability, so some shipping companies even added false stacks to appear bigger.

If I was a psychologist I guess I could add some clever remark about the size of a ship's smokestacks here, but I'm not, so let's move on!

Although the SS *Great Eastern*, first launched from Liverpool, England in 1858, had five stacks, it was still technically a hybrid because it also had sails. The first true four funnel steamship was the German SS *Kaiser Wilhelm der Grosse*. The Wilhelm first launched from Bremen, Germany in 1897 and like the Titanic later, the Wilhelm met an early demise when it was sunk by the British during World War I.

Since four funnel liners were expensive to operate, only fourteen were built from 1897 to 1922, with many, like the Wilhelm, being repurposed for World War I.

Unfortunately for the Titanic, she would never get that chance.

Olympic Class

As ocean liner companies competed to build the biggest and greatest ocean liners, the British based White Star Line company came up the with the idea of "*Olympic* Class" passenger steam ships. The idea was clearly a marketing gimmick, as it was just a name for its largest class of ships, the first of which was the *Olympic*. The Olympic launched in 1911 followed by the Titanic in 1912 and the *Britannic* in 1915.

The White Star Line billed their Olympic Class ships as the largest, fastest, and safest on the seas and the most luxurious if you could afford the first class ticket.

The White Star's Olympic Class liners were all built to similar specifications and each took about $7.5 million (approximately $200 billion in today's prices) to build. All were four funnel steamers that were powered by four cylinder reciprocating engines.

All of the Olympic class liners were about 900 feet long and about sixty-five feet deep. Each had nine decks, seven of which were for passengers, first, second, and third-class. The ships could carry over 3,000 passengers, but nearly 900 of those would be crew members on any voyage. The ships could usually go over thirty miles per hour in good weather.

One of the major selling points of the Olympic class ships were their state of the art design, which seemingly took into account most safety features.

Besides the thick hulls, each ship had an inner "skin" about the keel in case the outer hull should be breached. The ships were comprised of fifteen steel bulkheads in the lower decks that divided the hulls into sixteen watertight compartments. If the compartments were breached, there were electric pumps to eliminate the water and individual compartments could be sealed by automatic doors.

Theoretically, Olympic class ships could keep sailing with four compartments breached.

Although Olympic class ships were equipped with lifeboats, only twenty were installed on both the Olympic and Titanic because they were believed to have been nearly unsinkable due to the other safety precautions.

A Profitable Venture

It may help to view the golden age of ocean liners as you would the airline industry today. Since ocean liners were the only mode of transportation in which a person could travel around the world, there was quite a bit a money to be made building the ships and operating the lines.

The competition could be fierce and was primarily between British and

German companies. Both of those countries were wealthy and powerful in the late nineteenth and early twentieth centuries, and coincidentally they both sending many immigrants to America as well as Canada, Australia, and Argentina.

Building these ships was a titanic endeavor in itself (yes, pun intended) in terms of money, time, and manpower. The primary shipping building company in Britain was the Harland and Wolff company in Belfast, Northern Ireland. Harland and Wolff was started by Edward Harland and German born Gustav Wolff in 1861 in Belfast. The two men built a company that quickly became known for building the best ships in the world and was given most of the business by the White Star Line, most notably the construction of its Olympic Class ships.

Another notable British shipbuilding company was John Brown and Company, which built the RMS *Lusitania*.

But we'll get to her later. . .

There were also major ship building companies in Germany and France.

The companies that actually owned and operated the ocean liners were separate entities. As with the ship building companies, the major shipping companies were British and German, although there were also major French and Italian companies.

In Britain, the two major shipping companies were the Cunard Line and the White Star Line. The Cunard Line began in 1840 as a royal mail service owned and operated by Nova Scotian Samuel Canard. By the late 1800s, due to intense competition from other lines, the Cunard Line was forced to modernize its fleet of steamships and to offer a combination of luxury class travel and efficient passage for immigrants.

Cunard's primary rivals were the German companies Hamburg America Line and Norddeutscher Lloyd, but its biggest competition was from the British White Star Line.

The White Star Line began in 1845 when founders John Pilkington and Henry Wilson thought it would be a good way to capitalize on the Australian gold rush. By the late 1800s White Star Line executives learned that the true gold rush of that period was the immigration wave going to America, so they began to purchase steamers that could transport large numbers of immigrants to New York harbor.

The White Star Line's rise to the top of the shipping world was largely due to the vision of Thomas Henry Ismay (1837-1899), who took over the company in 1867. He successfully led the company from his Liverpool office, tremendously increasing its profits until he died and control of the company passed to his son, J. Bruce Ismay (1862-1937).

The White Star Line continued to be quite profitable with J. Bruce as its chairman, but Bruce had the unfortunate happenstance of being the head of the company when the Titanic sank.

He was also on board during the tragic voyage?

Did he survive? Keep reading to find out what happened!

The Belfast Harbour

The Belfast Harbour was first built in the seventeenth century, but it wasn't until the late eighteenth century when it became the premier port of the North Atlantic. The harbour itself was built on swamp land that had to be reclaimed by filling it with land and creating a series of canals and quays.

By the mid-1800s when the Harland and Wolff Company made the harbour their home, the port area covered several miles and consisted of several piers, quays, and scores of warehouses and factories.

When Harland and Wolff entered the scene, the company not only modernized the port, but also provided an economic boon to the city of Belfast that lasted for decades after the Titanic sank.

Most of the dock and port workers were from the Protestant east Belfast section, which also happened to be right next to the harbour. Workers lived with their families next to one another, walked to work together, and spent time in the corner pubs after work before returning home to their families.

The workers ranged from the more skilled and crew bosses to manual labors. All the workers had a sense of purpose and community, especially when Harland and Wolff announced the creation of the Olympic class ships.

Employment in the harbour soared while the Olympic and Titanic were being built, peaking at around 15,000 workers in 1911.

Although the vast majority of the men who built the ocean liners in the late 1800s and early 1900s never sailed on one, they took great pride in their work and were happy whenever one of their creations left the port.

They were also sad whenever they learned when one had been lost.

The Haves

The shipbuilders obviously made their profits by building and selling state of the art ships to shipping companies, but the shipping companies were dependent on one commodity to make profits—people.

Sure, the shipping companies were paid nicely for delivering mail across the oceans, but most of their money was made by delivering people. The companies developed a business model that utilized the concepts of both "quantity" and "quality," which by the time the Titanic sailed was an established part of the industry.

The "quantity" aspect involved packing as many immigrants as possible into the steerage section of the ship, which eventually evolved into third-class. Although third-class tickets were cheap compared to first and even second-class, they would consume a fair amount of a working-class man's savings. Many of the immigrants in third-class traveled as families, so a factory worker or miner from Ireland or Germany would have to pay for his and his entire family's journey.

We'll get to the third-class passengers a bit more later.

The second-class passengers were an interesting lot because they represented the growing middle class in Europe and North America. Second-class tickets on the Titanic were £13, which is approximately £1,123 in today's money, or close to $1,500 if you are an American!

Onboard the Titanic, second-class amenities were quite nice and comparable to first-class on smaller ocean liners. Second-class passengers had access to a library, the men had a smoking room, and there was shuffleboard on their deck.

Traditionally, most second-class passengers on ocean liners were men, with many of them being teachers, academics, civil servants, and members of the clergy. There were also a fair amount of pleasure cruisers in second-class.

But the true pleasure cruisers on the Titanic, and in all of the major ocean liners of the period, sailed in first class.

During the golden era of ocean liners, first-class travel was the only way to travel for Europe and America's elites. Robber barons, politicians, and the occasional gangster would rub elbows on the highest decks as they went from dinner to the ballroom or a Turkish bath.

First-class tickets were quite expensive on most ocean liners of the period and on the Titanic they included a wide range of prices. A single first-class ticket on the Titanic could set a person back £30 to £3,000 (about £3,000 to £85,000 in today's money or nearly $4,000 to $90,000)! First class passengers had access to exclusive bars and smoking rooms, gyms and health clubs, libraries, pools, baths, barbershops, and kennels for their pooches.

Because first-class passengers usually brought their servants along with them, there were often more of them than there were second-class passengers. There were 324 first-class passengers and 285 second-class passengers on the Titanic.

The rich and famous brought their opulent and privileged lifestyles with them on the high seas, but what was the voyage like for those in the bowels of the ship?

The Have Nots

Although third-class ocean liner passengers didn't travel in the same style as their first or even second-class counterparts, their living conditions were not so bad by the time the Titanic sailed. Third-class passengers may have been treated inhumanely in many ways when the first steam ships began ferrying immigrants across the seas in the nineteenth century, as they were often crowded into dormitory style quarters where disease and illness could rapidly spread, but by the early twentieth century that began to change.

Free enterprise often has a way of evening such things out, which is what happened in the case of third-class passenger accommodations.

As competition between the ship building and shipping companies became intense at the turn of the century, the White Star Line began offering better services and living quarters for third-class passengers. The Olympic class ships offered private cabins, public bathrooms, kitchens, a day room, and access to the poop deck. Generally speaking, third-class passengers were segregated from first and second-class passengers by grills and other barriers.

The actual chance of Jack and Rose getting together on the Titanic would've been remote.

As stated earlier, most third-class passengers on ocean liners were immigrants headed to the United States, Canada, Argentina, or Australia, depending on the route. The different nationalities were not segregated, but there were rarely ethnic problems on these long voyages—most travelers were looking forward to what lie ahead in their lives rather than the past.

Most of the third-class passengers on the Titanic were British and Irish, but there were also a number of Scandinavians, Germans, and eastern Europeans.

A third-class ticket onboard the Titanic was not cheap, either.

A single third-class ticket on the Titanic cost £7, about £680, or around $850. The Titanic's third-class facilities were the best of any ship and were superior to second-class facilities on many other lines.

Third-class passengers got what they paid for on the Titanic, at least up until the end.

Luxury or Speed?

As the competition for passengers heated up between the White Star and Cunard lines in the late 1800s and early 1900s, the companies focused on either luxury or speed. The White Start Line decided to focus on luxury first when it began construction of its Olympic class ships, although those ships were still certainly fast for the time and capable of traversing the Atlantic relatively quickly.

The Cunard Line decided to put speed slightly ahead of luxury. Its ships were certainly opulent, but their main selling point was their speed.

Like the White Star Line, the Cunard Line built a trio of four funnel steamships—the RMS *Lusitania*, the RMS *Mauretania*, and the RMS *Aquitania*—of which the first two went into service a few years before the White Star's Olympic class ships. Although the Cunard ships were big and nice, the designers wanted them to be the fastest to cross the Atlantic and in that respect their true competition was the German lines, not the White Star Line.

The ship that could cross the Atlantic the fastest was given the unofficial prize known as the "Blue Riband." The prize was generally held by German built and operated ships until the Lusitania took the prize in 1907 and 1908. The Mauretania then took the prize every year from 1909 until 1929 with a speed of just over twenty-six knots or thirty miles per hour, setting a record in the process.

The White Star ships may have been a little bigger and nicer than the Cunard ships, and the Cunard ships may have been a little faster, but the ships of both lines were overall very similar.

And neither line was immune from major maritime disasters.

The RMS *Lusitania*

If the Cunard Line was the White Star Line's rival company, then the Lusitania was the Titanic's rival as a ship.

For a time the Lusitania was the fastest ship in the world until it was eclipsed by its sister ship the Mauretania. In many ways, the Lusitania proved to be a template for the Titanic – it was a four funnel steamer that was the largest ship for a time.

The Lusitania was built partly with generous loans from the British government, which meant that it had to be built to Admiralty standards and possibly serve as a cruiser in war time.

With that said, the Lusitania was no drab vessel. Her technology was state of the art, which included wireless radio capability. Lusitania's passenger accommodations were also a step above what the other liners offered until the White Star Line launched its Olympic class ships. One of the features that the Lusitania introduced that was replicated by other ships, including the Titanic, was improved conditions for third-class passengers.

The Lusitania and the Titanic were for the most part cut from the same cloth and shared many features, but perhaps the most apparent thing the two ships shared was their tragic ends.

The Titanic sank tragically in 1912 and the Lusitania followed just over three years later on May 7, 1915. Although the Titanic's death was the result of a series of miscues that we will cover later, the Lusitania was the victim of a single torpedo by a German U-boat.

The death toll was immense—1,192 of the 1,960 passengers died, including 128 Americans.

A Ship a Week

The White Star Line's Olympic class liners were to supposed to be able to sail across the Atlantic Ocean in one week, which meant that when two were on the sailing at the time a person would only have to wait a week at the most to board one in either Southampton or New York.

The Olympic left on its maiden voyage from Southampton on June 14, 1911 and arrived in New York exactly one week later.

The Olympic continued to make voyages across the Atlantic for the following ten months, so that when the Titanic was finally launched in April 1912 the White Star Line would finally be able to put its "ship a week" plan into action.

When the Titanic ran into trouble the Olympic was heading the opposite way across the Atlantic and received the distress call from its sister ship, but it was too far to save any of the passengers.

Southampton to New York

The Titanic, and nearly every other White Star and Cunard ocean liners, left from the not so well-known English city of Southampton. Perhaps Southampton is known to you if you are British or have traveled in Britain, but it is not one of Britain's better known cities.

But for about a 100 year period it was among Britain's most important cities.

Southampton was a bit of a quiet coastal town until the Southampton Docks were built in 1835. From that point forward, the city grew around the increased sea traffic in and out of the city. Ships carrying cargo to and from Britain's many colonies filled the docks daily and when the golden age of steamships began in the mid-1800s the city became the primary British port for both the White Star and Cunard lines.

As with the people of Belfast, the residents of Southampton, known as Sotonians, took great pride in their connection to the sea. The Southampton Docks was the primary employer in the city during the late 1800s and early 1900s and residents were often highly represented as crews on the ocean liners.

Four out of five Titanic crew members made Southampton their home and Sotonians accounted for about one-third of all deaths from the tragedy.

Random Facts

1. Robert Fulton was commissioned by Napoleon Bonaparte to build the first true submarine—the *Nautilus*—in 1800.
2. Unlike the Titanic, the Olympic lived a long life, finally being retired in 1935 after twenty-four years of service.
3. Like most other ocean liners of the period, the Titanic's third-class section primarily held European immigrants, but there were also a small number of immigrants from the Middle East. Most of those passengers spoke Arabic but were Christian and came from countries such as Lebanon, Syria, and what is today Israel.
4. Chinese, Japanese, and Filipino immigrants comprised the majority of third-class on trans-Pacific ocean liners.
5. Although the White Star and Cunard lines came to dominant the passenger steamship industry in the late 1800s and early 1900s, the Inman Line was one of the first companies to offer upgraded third-class amenities to its customers.
6. Cargo planes for the most replaced ships as carriers of royal mail by the late twentieth century, but parts of the British Overseas Territory of Saint Helena, Ascension and Tristan da Cahuna are so isolated and without airstrips that mail is still delivered by RMS.
7. The political and religious instability in Ireland and Northern Ireland in the early twentieth century was especially pronounced in and around the city of Belfast, which affected the Harland and Wolff's business. Because of the instability, the company bought another shipyard in Glasgow, Scotland in 1912.
8. The White Star Line's primary German competitors were Norddeutscher Lloyd, which was based in Bremen, Germany, and the Hamburg American Line.
9. Due to social conventions of the time, women were prohibited from entering "smoking rooms" in the Titanic on all three passenger classes.
10. The top deck on the Olympic class ships was known as the Boat Deck. The life boats, wheelhouse and officer's quarters were on this deck. There was also a first-class lounge on this deck.
11. The A Deck or Promenade Deck was the level

immediately below the Boat Deck on all Olympic class ships. The Promenade Deck ran the entire length of the ship and contained first and second-class cabins, which following the standards of the time were separated from each other by partitions.

12.	Since there were far fewer ships using the south Atlantic routes and the area is considerably larger than the north Atlantic, there were less accidents and no major disasters in that region. The German Hamburg Süd line was one of the primary lines to operate in the south Atlantic, bringing immigrants from Germany to Argentina, Uruguay, and Brazil.

13.	The Belfast Harbour was originally started by a Royal Charter in 1613. The original wharf was built at the confluence of the small Lagan and Farset rivers near downtown Belfast.

14.	Belfast is part of the political entity known as Northern Ireland, which is part of the United Kingdom. Most Protestant-Unionists refer to the province as "Ulster."

15.	The British government formed the Belfast Harbour Commissioners in 1847. This government body was given wide-ranging powers to further modernize the Belfast Harbour by reclaiming more land and building more piers. The commissioners were also given more power to regulate trade and entice businesses, such as Harland and Wolff, to move to the Belfast Harbour.

16.	The Lusitania was named for a Roman province that included most of modern Portugal and part of southwestern Spain.

17.	During the golden era of the ocean liners, most ships were "christened" before their maiden voyages by upstanding members of society. The Lusitania was christened by Charlotte Burns, the Lady Inverclyde.

18.	The first and second-class accommodations on most ocean liners of the period, including the Titanic, included "writing rooms." Writing rooms were simply an extension of the library and were a place for the passengers to write letters or to do academic work. Since a number of the men in second-class on the Titanic and other Olympic class ships were academics, these rooms were used frequently.

19.	The SS Austria was operated by the Hamburg America

Line. Although the 1858 sinking of the ship was a disaster for the families and of the victims and the company, Hamburg America was able to bounce back and was one of the top ocean liner companies by the end of the century.

20.   A "poop deck" is the highest deck on a ship and usually forms the roof on a cabin on the stern. On older ships the helmsman would steer the ship from the quarter deck, which was just in front of the poop deck.

Test Yourself – Questions and Answers

1) What was Robert Fulton's nationality?

    a. American
    b. British
    c. German

2) How much did a single third-class ticket on the Titanic cost?

    a. £25
    b. £7
    c. £15

3) Where was the Titanic built?

    a. New York Harbor
    b. Bremen Harbor
    c. Belfast Harbour

4) How many smoke funnels did Olympic class ocean liner have?

    a. Two
    b. Three
    c. Four

5) What was the White Star Line's major British competitor?

    a. Hamburg America Line
    b. Cunard Line
    c. Krebs Line

Answers

1. a
2. b
3. c
4. c
5. b

CHAPTER TWO
THE IDEA OF THE TITANIC

It should be clear now that the Titanic was not built on a whim but was rather the culmination of decades of trial and error in the ocean liner industry. A number of factors had to come together to make it a reality and a number of men has to sacrifice their time, fortunes, and sometimes their lives to make the Titanic a reality.

Once the executives of the White Star Line and Harland Wolff decided that they would build the world's largest and most luxurious ocean liner and appropriately christen it, "Titanic," then it was just a matter of allocating the money and resources to the project.

An army of draftsmen and architects were hired to draw up the plans.

The Belfast Harbour needed specific upgrades.

And even more skilled and unskilled workers were needed to physically put the ship together.

Eventually, all of this happened within about a five year period.

An Ambitious Man

The late nineteenth and early twentieth centuries was a period in world history when ambitious men routinely made fortunes and legacies, sometimes at the expense of others. America was full of "robber barons" building railroads and opening mines, but plenty of these type of men could be found in Europe as well.

And many of them were in the shipping industry. William James Pirrie (1847-1924) was one such man.

Pirrie was born in Canada to a prominent Irish-Protestant family and was raised in his family's homeland of Northern Ireland. After graduating from the Royal Belfast Academical Institute, Pirrie joined Harland and Wolff as an apprentice, showing an incredible amount of drive, ambition, and intelligence.

Those were the days when those traits mattered perhaps more than anything, including who you knew.

Pirrie parlayed his success to become the chairman of Harland and Wolff in 1895 and he became the mayor of Belfast a year later. Although no one ever questioned Pirrie's civic pride, there is little doubt that his position as mayor helped the success of Harland and Wolff on the eve of its introduction of the Olympic class ships.

But conflicts of interest were never an issue in those days.

Pirrie assigned the primary architectural duties to his nephew, Thomas Andrews (1873-1912). Like his uncle, Andrews was a bright and ambitious man who was destined for big things in life. He oversaw work on the Olympic in 1907 and was rewarded for that by being given the lead on the construction of the Titanic in 1909.

When the Titanic was finally completed, uncle and nephew were proud of their accomplishment. Andrews was so proud of what he made that he insisted on making the Titanic's maiden voyage across the Atlantic.

An Army of Architects

Five years before the Titanic went on its fatal voyage, architects and draftsmen began drawing up the plans for the Titanic. Andrews' uncle was happy with his work on the Olympic, so he was rewarded with more pay and more workers.

Pirrie wanted his top architect to be happy and he also wanted to the Titanic to be a little better than the Olympic. It was, after all, going to be the largest passenger liner in the world so there was no reason why it shouldn't be the nicest.

And safest!

The general concepts of architecture and drafting were the same over 100 years ago as they are today, but some of the technology was obviously different. The Titanic's architects didn't have computers to aid their work, nor did they have small cameras or Xerox machines.

All of the Titanic's architects' work was hand drawn on linen rolls.

The architects and draftsmen worked in teams in large rooms at the Harland and Wolff facility in shifts. Hundreds of men worked long hours for several months until they submitted the plans of the Titanic and Olympic together to Bruce Ismay and the other directors of the White Star Line on July 29, 1908.

The board liked the plans and gave Harland and Wolff the green light to begin construction of both ships.

Queen's Island

Once the blueprints of the Titanic was accepted, Harland and Wolff executives immediately set about to begin construction. But since the construction of the Titanic and the Olympic was like nothing Harland and Wolff had done before, it required special circumstances.

The first thing that needed to be done was to figure *where* the massive Titanic was going to be built. Yes, the builders knew that it was going to be built in the Belfast Harbour, but there simply wasn't enough room to accommodate the construction of such large vessel, so Pirrie had to reclaim more land from the harbour.

Workers built a 185 acre artificial island that became known as Queen's Island to serve this purpose.

Queen's Island is where the Titanic and its two sister ships were slowly constructed and hundreds of workers spent a good share of their lives building the massive ships. Queen's Island continued to be used to build ships for decades after the Titanic's fateful journey, but it was never as great or important as it was from 1908 until 1912.

The Great Gantry

After Queens Island was made, the workers could finally start building the Titanic. It would take about three years, cost millions of dollars, and take the lives of several workers. The undertaking was clearly as big as the name, but if you are reading and happen to be a landlubber you are probably wondering: what do you build first?

They obviously just couldn't start by placing fabricated pieces together on the middle of the island, so the workers started by building a gigantic steel frame scaffolding, often known as a gantry, to assemble the ship.

And this was no ordinary gantry.

The Titanic's gantry, which became known as the "Great Gantry," was 840 feet long and 200 feet tall!

In other words, it would've dwarfed most building of the time and stood alongside the tallest buildings in most major cities.

Building the Great Gantry was a feat in itself, but once it was completed the workers could get to the real task at hand – building the Titanic.

Working on the Titanic

We've already covered some of the general working conditions and backgrounds of the Harland and Wolff harbour workers during the golden age of the ocean liners, so let's now take a look at some of what the Titanic workers specifically dealt with, saw, and could expect,

Needless to say, work on the Titanic could be physically and mentally exhausting.

There were hundreds of workers at any one time on the Titanic, hammering, riveting, and welding. The work could be physically taxing and extremely noisy, which was long before safety helmets, goggles, or any type of formal ear protection.

Some workers did improvise, though, by putting wads of Kleenexes in their hears to drown out the noise.

Although electricity was available for some things, it would've been impossible to provide enough artificial light for the entire gantry at the time so workers worked one sixteen hour shift Monday through Friday.

They also worked and eight hour shift every Saturday.

The workers would line up every day to receive a small wooden board that would record their breaks. They were only allowed seven minutes total for toilet breaks every day, which was closely monitored. Of course, such pressure was mentally exhausting for many of the workers.

Besides being physically and mentally demanding, working on the Titanic could be outright dangerous.

Nine men died over the course of building the ship and dozens more wore injured, sometimes permanently.

Still, despite the hardships, few of the Titanic workers complained. They were paid relatively well and each had a sense of pride and purpose in what they were doing. The men had the respect of their families and the city of Belfast so they did their utmost to make sure the ship was the best.

And as we'll see later, poor workmanship was not one of the reasons the Titanic sank.

Laying the Keel

Once the Great Gantry was built, the workers could finally set about to begin building the Titanic. The keel was the first thing to be made on the Olympic class liners as it was the backbone of those ships.

After the keel was placed, a frame clade in a steel hull was built on top of it.

With the skeleton of the Titanic complete, the workers then had to place tens of thousands of tons of steel into the frame. The steel was cut into individual plates about six feet wide and thirty feet long and fit into the hull.

From the bilge to the hull the plates were placed in an overlapping "clinkered" manner and from the bilge up they were placed used "strake" plating, which is essentially side by side placement.

The plates were kept in place by rivets.

Tools of the Trade

One of the interesting aspects the Titanic's construction was the fact that a combination of state of the art technology and time honored methods were used. The majority of the men who worked on the Titanic would've used simple tools, such as hammers, in their daily work.

Hammering a rivet doesn't require much technology, just some muscle and coordination.

But advanced technology was obviously required to move the large sheets of steel into place.

To move those sheets, large, steam powered cranes were built that could lift five tons of steel at a time. The massive cranes looked like something out of a steampunk story, but they were very effective and efficient—they were used in the Belfast Harbour for decades after the Olympic class ships were built.

There were other relatively new tools that the workers used to build the Titanic.

Arc welding was used for some small areas on the ship, but rivets were still used to secure the steel plates. Some hydraulic tools were used to move things as well, but the steam powered cranes were used for the majority of the larger pieces.

In total, it took 24,000 tons of steel and more than three million rivets to complete the hull of the Titanic. By May 1911, the Titanic was finally beginning to look like a real ship.

The Launching of the Hull

After two years of construction, the Titanic's hull was finally completed on May 31, 1911. The launching proved to be a major event, with all of the Harland and Wolff big wigs in attendance to make sure everything went as planned.

But things didn't go exactly as planned and perhaps they were an omen of bigger things to come.

The completed hull was encased in the Great Gantry—remember that thing? Well, the workers had to remove the Great Gantry before they could launch the hull, so that required disassembling the scaffolding piece by piece.

And since the hull was still encased in it, there was no quick and easy way of doing it. The steampunk cranes couldn't be used nor could any other tool or device that could've damaged the hull. The army of workers had to descend on the gantry and take it apart, piece by piece with hammers.

Although the job of removing the Great Gantry was relatively straight forward, it was somewhat dangerous. The workers would hammer pieces away from the scaffolding one at a time, but due to the structure's size there was an incredible pressure bearing down. The increased pressure meant that when some pieces were hammered away from the scaffolding they flew instead of fell.

One worker was killed by a flying piece of the Great Gantry.

But as tragic and foreboding as that worker's death may have been, the job needed to stay on schedule.

Adding the Engines

Once the Great Gantry was removed, the Titanic finally looked like a ship, but it was dead in the water without an engine, or engines.

The next task was adding the three engines to the ship, which were appropriately larger than what was used in most previous ships. The Titanic's two primary engines were reciprocating four cylinder steam engines. They were each thirty feet high and weighed an incredible 720 tons. The large, powerful engines had a combined output of 30,000 horsepower.

The reciprocating engines were seen as a step-up from turbine engines, as they were believed to be more reliable. But as a backup, there was also an auxiliary turbine engine.

Since the engines were steam powered, they needed to burn something to create that power. The Titanic had twenty-nine boilers that were heated by burning coal, which required the ship to carry nearly 7,000 tons in its bunkers. The ship required 600 tons of coal to be burned every day and 176 fireman working around the clock to shovel it into the furnaces. The ash was dumped into the sea and the steam was sent out three of the four funnels. The fourth was added partially to keep up with the Cunard Line's Lusitania, but it did provide ventilation for the kitchen.

The Titanic was finally ready for its finishing touches.

The Thompson Dry Dock

You've probably realized by now that everything associated with the Titanic, from the inception of its idea to its construction, was a monumental, titanic undertaking. After the Titanic's hull was finished and the engines were added, it would be almost another year before it would leave England on its fateful journey.

In order to put the final touches on the Titanic, it needed to be put into a dry dock.

But of course, not just any dry dock would do for the Titanic. The Thompson Dry Dock in the Belfast Harbour was the only facility that could handle such a big operation.

The Thompson Dry Dock, like many of the other construction apparatuses associated with the Titanic, was a bit of a marvel itself. It was nearly 900 feet long and 120 feet deep, making it one of the largest and only dry docks in the world at the time that could accommodate the Titanic. Also similar to the

Titanic, it took hundreds of workers six years to build the Thompson Dry Dock.

The Titanic was carefully piloted into the dry dock, the gates were closed, and then the water was pumped out of the dock.

The dry dock held about twenty-six million gallons of water, but due to state of the art pumping systems it only took about an hour and a half to completely drain the dock!

With the dock dry, work began on the Titanic's interior, which made it the ship that comes to everyone's minds.

Making it Functional

Although the Titanic was nearly done by the time it was put in the dry dock, it still needed a number of additions that would make it fully functional. Those additions would take almost another year to complete and thousands of more man hours.

The four funnels were added and of course the propellers had to be added to the engines. The ship was also painted, giving it its final, finished look.

But one of the final things added that made it truly a state of the art vessel was its wireless radio.

Wireless radio and telegraph communication grew out of telegraphic technology and became a reality in the late 1800s. Essentially, early wireless communication was a wireless version of the telegraph. You've probably seen an old western or "cowboys and Indians" film or television show where they communicated over long distances via telegraph, right? Well the type of communications system installed on the Titanic was basically the same thing, except that it didn't need the wires to send and receive messages.

Italian inventor Guglielmo Marconi (1874-1937) was the first person to create a commercially viable wireless telegraphy system and it was his company, "Marconi's Wireless Telegraph Company," that installed the wireless radio system on the Titanic.

The large radio needed separate rooms for the transmitter and the receiver because the noise from the transmitter interfered with the receiver. The Titanic's two radio operators, John Phillips and Harold Bride, were also Marconi employees.

Only one of the men would survive the tragedy.

The Ship's Interior

The Titanic was finally ready for the final round of work on its interior. It is perhaps ironic that that the interior work, which also happened to be the most detailed and "artistic" work, would be seen by so few and due to the sudden nature of the tragedy photographs are the only documentation of the interior.

Many of the artists who worked on the Titanic's interior also worked on Belfast's city hall, which was completed six years before the Titanic. A leisurely walk through Belfast's city hall will quickly bring to mind pictures of the Titanic's interior, especially the famous staircase.

The wooden staircase that descended from the promenade deck to the first-class dining room was the center piece of the Titanic and was the backdrop in many scenes from films about the tragic ship, including the 1997 *Titanic*.

Unfortunately, all of the excellent workmanship from the interior of the Titanic was forever lost. The Belfast city hall is the closest a person will ever get to the beautiful interiors of the doomed ship.

A Media Sensation

Today, we live in a society where as soon as things happen they are known to the world, becoming viral through any number of social media outlets. Although news wasn't disseminated quite as quickly in the early twentieth century, events as big as the construction of the Titanic were given serious media attention.

You might have seen headlines of the Titanic leaving Southampton and you've no doubt seen at least a couple of the reports of it sinking, but there were just as many stories written about its construction. Every step of the Titanic's construction was chronicled by media outlets from around the world.

Reports of the initial idea of the Titanic and its subsequent construction were published by the bigger name papers from London to Los Angeles and from Berlin to Chicago, but smaller newspapers also chronicled the endeavor.

"Monster Liners" was the title of a February 4, 1910 article in the *Desert Evening News* of Salt Lake City, Utah. The article detailed the idea and construction of the White Star Line's three Olympic class ships.

The Daytona Daily News of Daytona, Florida ran a somewhat wordy titled article, "The World's Largest Vessel, the Titanic, Now Being Built" on January 8, 1910. The article related many of the details of the Titanic's construction and dimensions we've discussed.

Some of the articles were a bit mundane and even silly, but reflect just how interested in the Titanic people of the world were at the time. The *British Daily Manchester Courier and Lancashire Advertiser*, a regional daily paper in England, reported in a October 11, 1911 article: " One of the funnels is erected in position, as also are the masts. As regards the state of things on some of the principal passenger desks, accommodation is very far advanced, and the work is proceeding towards completion speedily."

By the time the Titanic made its first sea trials, most people in the industrialized world knew something about the world's largest ship.

Ill Omens?

Throughout history, sailors have traditionally been a superstitious lot. The way flocks of birds fly, schools of fish swim, and the winds blow are among the things that have been viewed by mariners as good or bad omens of their voyages. But the Titanic was supposed to put an end to all of that with its new technology and everything, right?

Not everyone was convinced of the Titanic's ability to rise above old thinking and they were among the first people to point out that the issues pointing toward its ill-fated voyage.

The Titanic was supposed to begin its sea trials on April 2, 1912, but they were delayed for a day by bad weather. Most people thought nothing of the delay at the time—the capricious nature of the Irish Sea commonly delayed launches of ships. When the Titanic finally launched on its sea trials, its fathers, William Pirrie and Bruce Ismay, were unable to attend due to illness.

Still, despite two ill omens before the Titanic even conducted its sea trials, most people were more focused on getting her to Southampton.

The trials took place just outside of Belfast Harbour in the Irish Sea, lasting about twelve hours. The Titanic sailed just under 100 miles, reaching a maximum speed of twenty-one knots (twenty-four miles per hour) for an average of eighteen knots (twenty-one miles per hour). After the trials, the surveyor declared the Titanic seaworthy, which cleared her for the 660 mile voyage to Southampton.

She arrived in Southampton on April 4 and the ship's crew began arriving shortly thereafter to begin work.

The world's largest ship was finally ready to make its maiden voyage.

SS *Nomadic*

An often forgotten part of the Titanic's short life is the ship that was used to ferry people to her from continental Europe—the SS *Nomadic*.

You could call the Nomadic the little sister of the Titanic and Olympic, as it was built alongside them in the Belfast Harbour. The Nomadic is a 230 foot long, thirty-seven foot wide single funnel steamship that is still in existence. After the Nomadic was launched about a year before the Titanic, she spent the majority of her operating years in French waters piloted by a French crew. She had two decks for first and second-class passengers.

On April 10, 1912, the Nomadic left Cherbourg, France with 274 passengers for Southampton where they would all board the Titanic.

The Nomadic then went back to Cherbourg to live a long life, primarily as a civilian transport ship, but ferrying troops during both world wars. In the days, weeks, and months after the Titanic tragedy, the Nomadic was for the most part forgotten.

Random Facts

1. Although the technology on the Titanic was state of the art, wireless telegraphy was near the end of its life in 1912. Radio as we know it today quickly began replacing it in the following years.
2. The Titanic had three propellers for each engine. Each of the propellers stood nearly twenty-four feet and weighed thirty-eight tons.
3. Although Harland and Wolff overwhelming hired Protestant workers, they would occasionally hire Catholics, but they often didn't last long. Catholic workers were subject to subject to daily harassment and some claimed to have had rivets nearly dropped on them from above.
4. The fire men who shoveled the coal on the Titanic were known as the "black gang" due to usually being covered in coal.
5. William Pirrie planned to be on the Titanic's maiden voyage, but illness kept him home and saved his life. He was questioned numerous times throughout his life about the lack of life boats on the Titanic.
6. The Titanic had 26,800 cubic feet of space in her holds for mail. Three American and two British postal workers were on the voyage to sort tens of thousands of pieces of mail.
7. Contrary to the 1997 film, the most valuable item onboard the Titanic was a 1814 oil painting titled *La Circassieme au Bain* by Merry-Joseph Blondel. The painting's owner, Swede Hakon Steffanson, survived the tragedy and filled a claim for $100,000 or about $2.5 million in today's money.
8. The men who built the Titanic were not unionized.
9. The Titanic's funnels were painted a yellowish color known as "White Star bluff" that was used exclusively on White Star Line ships.
10. In what many consider to be another odd twist in the short and tragic life of the Titanic, it was never christened. Although most ocean liners of this ere were christened before their maiden voyages, it was the policy of the White Star Line not to do so.

11.	Work on the Thompson dry dock began in 1904 and was completed in time for the final work on the Titanic.

12.	Most of the rivets were put into the ship manually with hammers, although some were placed using hydraulic tools.

13.	The anchors were the last pieces to be added to the ship. The Titanic had two side anchors and a middle anchor. The middle anchor was the largest ever made, weighing in at sixteen tons.

14.	Although the Titanic was built in Belfast and sailed from Southampton, Liverpool was its registered home port. Liverpool was the traditional British port of call for the White Star Line until the early 1900s when it moved to Southampton.

15.	The Nomadic was officially a "tender" ship. Tender ships serve exclusively, or almost exclusively, to transport goods and people to larger ships.

16.	Thomas Andrews had a wife and two-year-old daughter when the Titanic sailed.

17.	Pirrie's brother-in-law, Alexander Carlisel (1854-1926), was the draftsman primarily responsible for designing the safety systems on the Titanic, which included the life boats. He quit working on the Olympic class ships in 1910 because he disagreed with Pirrie on the number of life boats required for each ship—he thought there should be enough ships for every passenger.

18.	American tycoon John Pierpont Morgan Senior (J.P. Morgan) played a not so small role in the creation of the Titanic. He helped finance the International Mercantile Marine Company (IMMC), which had several subsidiary companies, one of which was the White Star Line. The Titanic disaster led to the IMMC going bankrupt and Morgan died about a year later.

19.	The Titanic's rudder was nearly eighty feet high and fifteen feet long and weighed over 100 tons.

20.	The Titanic had its own electrical plant that was equivalent to an average city's power station of the period. It had four primary generators and two backups, which like with most things on the Titanic, were powered by steam.

Test Yourself – Questions and Answers

1. What was the name of the artificial island where the hull of the Titanic was constructed?
    a. King's Island
    b. Duke's Island
    c. Queen's Island

2. Which of these cities was *not* directly connected to the Titanic?
    a. Belfast
    b. Southampton
    c. London

3. How many engines did the Titanic have?
    a. Three
    b. Two
    c. One

4. What was the religious background of the vast majority of the Titanic's workers?
    a. Catholic
    b. Protestant
    c. Jewish

5. Much of the Titanic's interior was modeled after the city hall of what city?
    a. Belfast
    b. Paris

    c. Kansas City

Answers

1. c
2. c
3. a
4. b
5. a

CHAPTER THREE
LEAVING PORT

When the Titanic left the port of Southampton on April 10, 1912 it was filled with 1,300 passengers and 885 crew. As the passengers waved goodbye to their friends and family in Southampton, there was definitely a sense of optimism wafting through the air. The people knew they were going to be part of history.

Unfortunately for them, they became part of history in a different way than they intended.

In the fascinating story of the Titanic, the crew and passengers each had their own stories. The blend of first, second, and third-class passengers, along with some interesting crew members, could be enough for several books and movies alone. The passengers ranged from one of the richest men in the world to poor immigrants who used their life savings for a ticket aboard the world's largest boat and a chance to make something of themselves in America.

In the five days before tragedy struck, passengers made new friends and business deals, enjoyed the luxurious amenities of the ship, and many just took the time to forget about all their troubles back in Europe or America.

The average passenger and crew on the Titanic was truly happy to be part of history.

The Guarantee Group

Among the crew members of the Titanic that left Southampton were nine men known as the "Guarantee Group." These men were Harland and Wolff ship workers from Belfast who were specially chosen to go on the maiden voyage of the Titanic by Thomas Andrews as a sort of working vacation.

Before leaving Belfast, Andrews instructed his four best men to pick four apprentices who would record the trip and do any troubleshooting if need be.

Andrews, electrician William Parr, and draftsman Roderick Chisholm were given first-class accommodations, while the rest of the men sailed in second-class.

Besides Andrews, Parr, and Chisholm, the Guarantee Group included: joiner William Campbell; machinists Alfred Cunningham, Anthony Frost, and Robert Knight; plumber Francis Parkes; and electrician's apprentice Ennis Watson.

Being chosen for the Guarantee Group was an honor among the workers and considered to be basically a bonus and an incentive for the workers to do their best. Although the Guarantee Group members were on call during the voyage, they were free to enjoy the trip and all of the ship's amenities.

All of the Guarantee Group went down with the ship and their remains were never recovered.

The Richest Man in the World

The first-class passenger list of the Titanic was a veritable who's who of Europe and America's elite. European nobility, American tycoons, and politicians from both sides of the Atlantic rubbed elbows on the promenade decks, dinned, and danced with each other into the early morning hours. Among the elite passengers was the man who was quite possibly the riches in the world—John Jacob Astor IV.

Astor was born into the Astor family, who earned their millions by trading in furs and making excellent real estate deals. By the time Astor boarded the Titanic, he was forty-seven-years-old and worth nearly $90 million or nearly $2.5 billion in today's money.

He was also a man who had accomplished much more than inheriting family money.

He used his family money to make several lucrative real estate deals, which included building the world famous Waldorf-Astoria Hotel. He received patents on several minor inventions and wrote a science fiction book, *A Journey to Other Worlds,* which was published in 1894. He married his first wife, an East Coast blue blood named Ava Willing, in 1891 and had two sons with her.

But as so often happens with powerful men, Astor's attention turned to a younger socialite.

A much younger socialite.

Astor divorced his wife in 1909 and remarried eighteen-year-old Madeline Force in 1912. The nearly thirty year age difference between the couple and the fact that Astor appeared to leave his wife for his young paramour turned wife caused quite a stir among polite East Coast society—so much so that the couple decided to take an extended honeymoon in Egypt and Europe.

As is often the case, especially back then, Madeline became pregnant during their extended honeymoon and together the couple agreed that it would be best if their child was born in America. The Astors, along with their beloved Airedale terrier Kitty, and a nurse, a maid, and a valet, boarded the Titanic along with thousands of other hopeful passengers.

When tragedy finally struck, only one of the Astors would survive.

Hanging Out in First-Class

As we discussed earlier, first-class was an exceptional experience on most ocean liners, but on the Titanic it was extraordinary! The first-class passengers had a wide range of luxuries and amenities to choose from and were given the best decks on the ships.

First-class passengers were housed in the A and B decks of the Titanic, which were the second and third highest decks on the ship. The A deck was also the promenade deck and featured a number of first-class cabins, lounges, and other amenities. The B deck was much longer and therefore had a combination of first and second-class amenities.

There were actually first-class facilities all the way down to the F deck, which essentially gave the first-class passengers the run of the ship.

There were also a select number of large first-class cabins on the B deck known as "staterooms." The staterooms were the equivalent of penthouses and each had its own promenade. After all, the richest of the Titanic's couldn't be expected to mix with the great unwashed when they were viewing the ocean, even if it was other rich people, right?

The Astor family was staying in one of the staterooms.

One of the facilities that many of the health conscious first-class passengers took advantage of was the ship's gymnasium. For those of you who work out know, exercise often follows trends and its also often dependent or influenced by technology. The Titanic's gym was no different. There were no free weights in the Titanic's gym as weight lifting was regarded as an extreme activity at the time, but there were rowing machines, punching bags, exercise bikes, and other cardiovascular machines.

The gymnasium was strictly segregated by gender and only available to first-class passengers.

There was also a Turkish bath, a small swimming pool, and a squash court available to first-class passengers on a per use fee basis.

Besides the palatial ball room, first-class passengers also access to a number of bars, cafes, smoking rooms, and writing rooms located on various decks throughout the ship.

The first-class passengers could access all of these facilities, from the A to the E deck, via the Grand Staircase. You've probably seen the Grand Staircase replicated in fictional or documentary accounts of the Titanic because the six flight stairs were definitely impressive in terms of size and style. The Grand Staircase was the central nerve of the Titanic's first-class social activity—business deals, friendships, and even a couple of romances were made on the Grand Staircase, although unfortunately most of them were short lived.

Because the first-class facilities were on most of the decks of the ship, the first-class passengers would from time to time rub elbows with the second-class passengers.

Second-class passengers like Lawrence Beesley.

Lawrence Beesley

Among all the second-class passengers, perhaps none were more interesting than Lawrence Beesley and certainly not as well-documented.

Lawrence Beesley was born in 1877 in Derby, England to a middle class family. He was a true bookworm from an early age, choosing reading and scientific observation over sports and athletics. He became a science teacher, married a woman named Gertrude in 1901, and had a son with her in 1903.

Everything seemed to going well for the studious Beesley until his wife died of respiratory disease in 1906. Beesley continued to work and care for his son, but he was lost without his wife. At the suggesting of friends and family, Beesley decided to leave his son with family and take a prolonged visit to North America. He planned to visit a number of places in the United States as well as his brother in Toronto, Ontario.

He bought a second-class ticket on the Titanic for the trip.

Although sociable, Beesley spent much of his time in his cabin reading, which is where he was and what he was doing when tragedy struck.

Lawrence Beesley would later play a major role in how the tragedy of the Titanic was remembered, so we'll get back to him later.

Second-Class Accommodations

As mentioned earlier, second-class lodgings and accommodations on the Titanic were quite nice relatively speaking and equal to first-class on some of the smaller ocean liners of the era. Second-class facilities were locate on decks B through F with most of the cabins on decks B, E, and F. For the most part, second-class accommodations mirrored those of first-class, except they tended to be smaller and less luxurious.

Like with first-class, the second-class passengers had a variety of different cabin options and varying scale of cost. There were second-class "staterooms" that also doubled as lower tier first-class cabins, which demonstrates that even a middle-class experience on the Titanic was a step above the rest.

Second-class passengers had access to three promenade decks, including the boat deck where all of the lifeboats were kept. It's hard not to think that a least a few of the second-class passengers who were taking leisurely strolls on the boat deck took a look at those lifeboats and wondered if there were enough of them.

The second-class library was of considerable size, probably because it had to also function as the second-class drawing and writing rooms and lounge. It was a place where both second-class men and women could mix freely.

Some of you reading this may find it hard to believe, but in the pre-Internet era libraries usually served a variety of functions, one of which was as a social gathering place. When Lawrence Beesley wasn't in his room reading or writing, he was either doing the same in the ship's library or there making new friends.

The second-class dining hall, usually known as the "dining saloon," was considerably smaller than its first-class counterpart, but still larger than the first-class accommodations of other ocean liners of the time. It could seat nearly 400 guests at one time.

Among the second-class passengers were many of the Titanic's crew.

The Wallace Hartley Band

If you've seen any fictional version of the Titanic disaster, no doubt the band featured prominently at some point. In many of these renditions the band is little more than a minor plot device, playing in the background as the main characters explore the ship and live the last few days of their lives.

But as the ship is sinking, the band is often featured more prominently, playing songs until the very end.

There were actually two bands on the Titanic. The primary band was a five piece led by Wallace Hartley, with bassist John Clark, violinist John Hume, and cellists Percy Taylor and John Woodward. The other band was a three piece comprised of violinist Georges Kirns, cellist Roger Bricoux, and pianist Theodore Bailey. The Wallace Hartley Band played the larger rooms, while the smaller band played in the ship's first class bars.

All of the musicians were British, with the exception of Bricoux, who was French.

The musicians were not employees of either Harland and Wolff or the White Star Line, but worked under contract for the White Star Line through a music agency. All of the men stayed in second-class cabins.

Although the details of what took place with the musicians after the Titanic hit that fate full iceberg will forever remain a mystery, many of the survivors reported that they kept playing until the very end. Because of their efforts to ease the chaos of the situation, the Titanic's musicians have been remembered as heroes, with one memorial built for them in Southampton and two in Australia.

All of the Titanic's musicians perished in the sinking.

A Not So Indiscrete Traveler

Benjamin Guggenheim's life mirrored that of fellow traveler Jacob Astor in many ways. Although Astor's family was Christian and Guggenheim came from a Swiss-Jewish family, both men were born into obscenely large amounts of money and both were about the same age when they boarded the Titanic—Guggenheim was forty-six and Astor was forty-seven. Both men were also part of the East Coast American elite and their names were both well known around America, then and now.

Yes, Benjamin was the brother of Solomon Guggenheim, the guy who founded the Guggenheim Museum in New York.

And perhaps most interesting, both men left their wives for women much younger than them. Astor married his nearly thirty year younger girlfriend,

while Guggenheim was traveling with his eighteen years young paramour—
Léotine Aubart.

Aubart was as interesting as she was exotic, which was no doubt what
attracted the tycoon to her. After Guggenheim's marriage to his wife Florette
became loveless, he began spending more time in his Paris apartment, which
is where he met the French singer Aubart. The two quickly began a
passionate affair and perhaps due to the fact that they were living in the much
more permissive France, were not afraid to be public about their relationship.
In fact, there were rumours that Guggenheim was bringing Aubart to the
United States because he was planning to divorce his wife.

Whether that is true or not will never be known.

Like Astor, Guggenheim was traveling with a chauffeur, valet, and maid in
addition to his mistress.

When the tragedy finally struck, Guggenheim saw Aubart to a lifeboat and
then went with his valet, Victor Giglio, back to their cabin where they
changed into their evening formal wear. The two men then went to the Grand
Staircase where they were last seen sipping brandy and smoking cigars with
some other men from first-class.

Guggenheim's body was never recovered.

Rhoda Abbott

Not all of the interesting and tragic stories from the Titanic came from the
first-class section. There were 706 third-class passengers, which was nearly
equal to the number of passengers in first and second-class combined, so
there was certainly some interesting and tragic cases from among them, right?

One of them was a young single mother named Rhoda Abbott.

Rhoda was far from a conventional woman of the period: she was a world
traveler, divorced, and later raised her children as a single mother. Hers is
definitely an interesting story.

Abbott was born Rhoda Hunt in 1873 in England but immigrated to the United States in 1893. While living in Providence, Rhode Island, Rhoda fell in love with a charismatic professional boxer named Stanton Abbott. The couple wed in 1895 and had two sons, Rossmore and Eugene. Rhoda quickly fell into the domestic life of a middle class American housewife, but her relationship with Stanton deteriorated.

The conflicts eventually led to a divorce in 1911, which was a relatively rare thing in the era long before no-fault divorces.

As tough as being a single mother can be today, you can about imagine what it would've been like for Rhoda Abbott in 1911. The social stigma alone would have been intense and very stressful, but it was also decades before public assistance and social safety nets were in place.

Most single mothers had to rely on their extended families for support. But Rhoda's family was back in England.

Rhoda and her two teenage sons sailed to England on board the Olympic, but life in the Old Country was simply not what she thought it'd be. She made little money and her sons, who were born and raised as Americans, felt like foreigners in their mother's native land. So Rosa bought three third-class tickets on board the Titanic to go back to America.

When the tragedy struck, Rosa and her sons were slow reacting to the situation and by the time they got to the top deck there was only one lifeboat left and not enough room for all of them.

Only one member of the Abbott family would survive.

Down in Steerage

Rhoda Abbott and her sons found themselves in quite different conditions on board the Olympic and Titanic than they would've had they taken the trip ten years prior. Although Titanic's third-class lodgings were located on the lower decks, it was not technically considered steerage because the passengers were housed in ten person cabins, not a dormitory as was common in steerage during the era.

Third-class facilities were located from the C Deck to the G Deck and included open spaces, a smoking room, and a dining saloon. The smoking room, as with the first and second-class versions, was only available to men and included a bar. The dining saloon was actually quite nice and large compared to other ocean liners of the period; it could accommodate 473 people at a time.

As nice as the third-class facilities on the Titanic were compared to other liners, since it was located close to the bowels of the ship it could be quite noisy. The accommodations were also the smallest in size, although the third-class passengers made up the majority of the Titanic's passengers.

The third-class passengers were segregated from the first and second-class passengers by a number of gates on every level. Although there was some mingling among the first and second-class passengers, there was virtually none by third-class passengers and the rest of the ship. The White Star Line justified this segregation partially because the third-class passengers were largely immigrants who had to pass through quarantine upon arrival in the United States.

They wouldn't want the steerage passengers to pass something on to their tycoon customers, would they?

There was also the fact that the world was much more class conscious over 100 years ago, especially in Europe. It was just the way things were and was never something that was challenged.

The third-class passengers were more concerned about making it to America than in challenging any social norms of the day.

The First Tabloid Journalist

Long before Geraldo Rivera had his nose broken by an angry skinhead, William Thomas Stead was reporting on some of the hottest topics of the nineteenth century and putting his life and liberty in jeopardy in the process. When the sixty-two-year-old Stead went down with the Titanic, he was not among the richest men in first-class, but he was probably one of the better known.

Stead was born into a religious family in England in 1849, which influenced his moralistic writings in his lifelong career as a journalist, mixing opinion and sensationalism freely.

He wrote a series of newspaper articles in 1885 titled "The Maiden Tribute of Modern Babylon," which outlined some of the sordid sex and crime taking place on the mean streets of Victorian London.

Stead later combined his journalism with his political beliefs of pacifism, criticizing his government for its war with the South African Boers and attempting to persuade the Tsar of Russia to follow a more peaceful course in world affairs. His blend of advocacy and proto-tabloid journalism earned him fans and enemies alike and eventually the recognition of American President William Howard Taft. The president had arranged an international peace conference at Carnegie Hall and had invited Stead to speak.

Stead bought a first-class ticket on the Titanic and quickly made friends among the ship's elite, thrilling them with stories about his time in jail, meeting the tsar, and moving among the dregs of London.

When the Titanic was sinking, Stead helped a number of women and children get safely into lifeboats.

He was last seen alive with Jacob Astor, clinging to a lifeboat. The cold water sapped all his strength, sending him to the bottom of the ocean.

William Thomas Stead's body was never recovered.

The Thinking Machine

Among the more notable non-tycoon Americans in first-class was journalist and mystery novelist Jacques Futrelle. Jacques was born in 1875 in rural Georgia to a middle-class family. The young Futrelle show an early aptitude for writing and storytelling, which eventually landed him numerous positions with East Coast newspapers in the late 1800s. The income allowed him to get married and start a family, but as an ambitious young man he wanted more.

But Jacques Futrelle's true passion was with fictional writing, particularly crime drama and mysteries. Futrelle developed a character named Professor Augustus S.F.X. Van Dusen, also known as the "Thinking Machine," to be the primary protagonist in fifty-one short stories and two novels. Although the Thinking Machine was compared to Sherlock Holmes, the character became extremely popular in the United States, earning Futrelle a degree of fame and financial security.

With the proceeds made from his Thinking Machine stories, Futrelle did as all of the good American writers of this time did—he took an extended trip to Europe.

Futrelle took his wife and fellow journalist, Lily May, with him on his trip, which they planned to end in grand fashion on board the Titanic. When the tragedy struck, Futrelle made sure that his wife was safely on one of the lifeboats.

She last saw him smoking a cigarette, talking to Jacob Astor.

Cheating Death?

Along with the Astors and Guggenheim, the Vanderbilt family was one of the most recognized and wealthy families in the early twentieth century. The Vanderbilts made their initial fortunes in railroads and then used that wealth to invest in a number of other lucrative business ventures. They then went on to fund a number of charities and non-profit organizations, the most famous of which is Vanderbilt University in Nashville, Tennessee.

Scheduled to sail on the Titanic was Alfred Gwynne Vanderbilt.

Upon the death of the Vanderbilt family patriarch in 1899, Alfred inherited most of the family's wealth. The money allowed Alfred to travel and enjoy life as he continued to build his family's wealth.

In 1912, Alfred was in Europe on business and pleasure when it is believed he bought a first-class ticket on board the Titanic to return to America. The reason why he didn't board the Titanic and if the ticket actually belonged to one of his relatives remains unclear, but what happened next is quite clear.

In another eerie coincidence linking the Titanic and Lusitania eternally together, Alfred died on the sinking of the Lusitania.

Vanderbilt may have been able to cheat death once, but not twice!

Two Last Stops

After leaving Southampton on April 10, the Titanic made a quick jaunt across the English Channel to Cherbourg, France where it picked up some supplies and some more passengers. Many of the passengers who got on in France were third-class passengers from continental Europe who didn't speak English. The Titanic then sailed back across the English Channel and made another stop in Queenstown (now Cobh), Ireland to pick up some more second and third-class passengers.

With the circuitous route out of the way, the Titanic was free to make its first journey across the Atlantic.

And apart from a couple of possibly ill omens in Belfast, the weather seemed to bode well for the trip. The skies were clear, the sun was shining, and the temperatures were mild, in the high 50s to low 60s Fahrenheit.

The passengers took full advantage of the weather by using the promenade and poop decks to socialize and enjoy the trip. By April 14, though, the Titanic had entered a cold front and the temperatures dropped so that by nightfall it was only in the upper 30s.

Still, the skies were clear and nearly everyone on board was thinking about docking in New York than any potential trouble that was ahead.

Captain Edwin Smith

No discussion about the passengers on board the Titanic would be complete without talking about the ship's captain, Edwin Smith. Captain Edwin Smith was a career sailor who got his start in the British Navy and can best be summed up as "an old salt dog."

By 1880, Smith was commanding ships for the White Star Line and had built a nice career and reputation for himself by the turn of the century. He was married with a daughter and lived in Southampton where he was close to the sea and the White Star Line ships he piloted. He was eventually given the responsibility of sailing the White Star Line's newest ships in 1904, but by 1911, at the age of sixty, Smith's age was beginning to show.

He was by then truly an *old* salt dog.

Today, sixty is not considered very old and even in 1911 it was below the average lifespan for most people in the industrialized world. With that said, there is a reason why certain professions force retirement on their employees beginning at age sixty, safety of course being the prime concern.

There is no doubt that our reflexes begin to diminish before the age of sixty.

And for Captain Edwin Smith that became apparent on September 20, 1911.

On that day Smith was piloting the Olympic when it collided with a British naval cruiser, the HMS *Hawke*. No one was hurt on either ship, but the Olympic suffered a broken propeller shaft and water entered one of her compartments, which forced Smith to bring her back to Southampton and eventually Belfast for repairs. Although Smith was not totally to blame for the incident, the Navy believed the Olympic crew was at fault for getting too close to their vessel.

Smith just didn't react quick enough and the immense size of the Olympic sucked the Hawke closer, creating the collision.

The accident cost the White Star Line and Harland and Wolff money and questions were raised about Smith's competency, but it was apparently not enough because he was given command of the Titanic.

The Last Supper

As you've been reading this you've probably gotten the sense that the Titanic passengers and crew were enjoying their trip and that no one had any idea of what was ahead. Things went on as they did for the first four days of the trip until the ship hit that iceberg.

For the first-class passengers, it meant having their final meal on the evening of April 14.

The first-class passengers assembled in the dining room that evening wearing their best suits and dresses. As with all of the previous evening, the passengers were treated to a sumptuous ten course meal, prepared by some of the best chefs in the world.

The Titanic's culinary crew included 113 cooks, fifteen head cooks, twelve pastry chefs, six bakers, five butchers, and five sous chefs.

The kitchen crew served not only the first-class passengers, but also the second and third-class passengers as well, although the fare varied considerably from class to class. Since many of the second-class passengers were middle class Americans, the meals reflected that with healthy servings of beef and turkey. There was also a happy hour in second-class for Americans who liked a drink before their meals.

The biggest third-class meal of the day was usually lunch, which was common among the British and Irish working class of the period.

But of course, the first-class dining, due to its opulence, grandeur, and some would say decadence, has attracted the most attention in the 100 plus years since the Titanic sank.

In case you were wondering, the last meal that Astor, Guggenheim, Stead, and the other passengers in first-class enjoyed included oysters, filet mignon, poached salmon, chicken Lyonnaise, foie gras, roasted pigeon, lamb with mint sauce and Punch Romaine, a palate-cleansing ice flavored with oranges and drenched in champagne.

It was definitely quite the last meal!

Random Facts

1. The Titanic required more than 75,000 pounds of fresh meat, 40,000 eggs, 36,000 apples, and 15,000 bottles among other provisions to feed its passengers and crew. The passengers and crew used more than 14,000 gallons of drinking water every day.
2. As a result of William Thomas Stead's investigative journalism into the seedy side of Victorian England, the British Parliament passed a law raising the age of legal sexual consent from thirteen to sixteen. The law became known unofficially as the "Stead Act."
3. The Titanic was only in Cherbourg for less than two hours. It left Queenstown/Cobh on April 11 at 1:30 pm., which means that it was only on the open sea for about eighty-two hours.
4. Guglielmo Marconi, the owner of the wireless company that provided the Titanic's wireless system, was scheduled to sail on the Titanic but instead took the Lusitania across the Atlantic days earlier.
5. John Jacob Astor's sister Helen married diplomat James Roosevelt, who was the half-brother of future President Franklin Delano Roosevelt.
6. The third-class dinner (served at lunch time) on April 14 included fresh bread, biscuits, fresh roast beef with brown gravy, sweet corn, fruit, and plum pudding. Not too bad!
7. Before leading the Titanic band, Wallace Hartley played with the Huddersfield Philharmonic Orchestra and the Cunard Line. His work with the Cunard Line brought him to the Lusitania, which served as yet another connection between the two doomed passenger liners.
8. Second-class passengers had a choice of main dishes for dinner, which included curried chicken for the British passengers, spring lamb, and roast turkey for the American and Canadian passengers.
9. Although Captain Edward Smith was born and raised in landlocked Staffordshire, England, he moved to Liverpool and

began his seafaring career at age seventeen.

10. Jacques Futrelle's mother, Linnie, died just over three months after her son perished in the Titanic disaster. Linnie was extremely close to Jacques and was said to have died from a broken heart.

11. A bugler would walk about and down the decks of the Titanic playing his horn to signal meal times.

12. There were 126 children, age fourteen or below, on board the Titanic.

13. Squash is more commonly known as racquet ball in the United States today.

14. Besides the social mores of the time that kept the third-class passengers from the first and second-class passengers, American immigration law also required it. Since the vast majority of third-class passengers were immigrants, they needed to be checked at Ellis Island before being released into the interior. First and second-class passengers could leave at the pier.

15. Although there were gates that separated the third-class passengers from the other passengers, the size of those gates has been misrepresented in many fictional accounts. The gates were about waist high and watched by stewards, but the stewards left their posts to go above when disaster struck.

16. American businessman and founder of the Hersey candy company, Milton S. Hershey, had bought a ticket for a stateroom on the Titanic but cancelled the trip to take care of business in Europe.

17. Although the third-class passengers were treated to lunches that were generally better than what they were used to, many opted to skip the evening meal. It was a sort of mystery dish known as gruel.

18. Queenstown, Ireland changed its name to the more Gaelic sounding Cobh in 1920 as the country was moving closer to independence from Britain.

19. Léotine Aubart claimed to have brought six trunks filled with more than twenty-four pairs of shoes and scores of shirts, dresses, and hats for the less than one week journey.

20.   Robert Chisholm was the oldest member of the Guarantee Group at age forty.

Test Yourself – Questions and Answers

1) Before finally embarking on its trans-Atlantic voyage, the Titanic stopped in which of these countries?
   - a. Scotland
   - b. Ireland
   - c. Germany

2) The "Guarantee Group" was a group of what?

   - a. Harland and Wolff's best employees
   - b. Industrialists
   - c. Politicians

3) This man was one of the richest, if not the richest, man in the world at the time and a passenger/victim on the Titanic?

   - a. Johan Jacob Astor IV
   - b. Robert Guggenheim
   - c. The Sultan of Brunei

4) How many bands played on the Titanic?

   - a. One
   - b. Five
   - c. Two

5) He was the captain of the Titanic?

   - a. Edward Smith
   - b. William T. Stead
   - c. Merrill Stubing

Answers

1 b
2 a
3 a
4 c
5 a

CHAPTER FOUR
TROUBLE AHEAD

By now you probably know more about the background of the Titanic than the average person. You know about the historical background of steamships and the golden age of ocean liners, how the Titanic was built, and a little bit about the background of the passengers and what their trip was like before tragedy struck.

But all of that is only half the story.

Technically, what we've covered so far makes up a far larger time span than the rest of this book, but what happened right before the Titanic hit that iceberg is an important story in itself.

From the time the Titanic struck the iceberg at around 11:40 pm local time until it sank beneath the waves of the icy North Atlantic, only about two-and-a-half hours had elapsed. Most people who know little about the Titanic may think that should've been enough time to get all of the passengers safely off the ship. But you know that there were quite a few passengers to evacuate, so an orderly evacuation would've taken time.

And once it was apparent that the ship was going down, order left on the first lifeboat!

The problem is that there were a number of factors and events that took place right before, during, and after the Titanic hit the iceberg that combined to create a perfect storm of mass carnage. One could call it a comedy of error if it weren't such a tragic event, but few there or who were living at the time found any humor in the sinking of the Titanic.

Iceberg Alley

The Atlantic Marine Ecozone, better known colloquially as "Iceberg Alley," is an area of the North Atlantic Ocean known for its deep stretches of water and hundreds to thousands of icebergs of varying sizes floating around at any given time. The area stretches from the Davis Strait, which is between Greenland the Canadian territory of Nanavut, down to the Grand Banks off the coasts of the Canadian provinces of Newfoundland and Nova Scotia.

Along with the hazards of icebergs, mariners traversing Iceberg Alley have also had to historically deal with heavy fog caused by the cold waters.

Because of all these factors, only sailors with sharp reflexes usually make the voyage and even they usually do so in a very conservative manner—it doesn't pay to try to rush through Iceberg Alley.

Iceberg Alley was no place for a sixty-one-year-old captain with recent history of accidents.

An Ancient Iceberg

Of all the characters in the Titanic saga, perhaps the most overlooked and underappreciated is the iceberg that the ship hit. We'll call said iceberg—the Iceberg. I mean, come on, doesn't it deserve some respect? It sort of did have a personality and it certainly had a backstory worth exploring.

So let's take a look at the "Iceberg."

The Iceberg, like 90% of the other icebergs in iceberg alley, came from the glaciers of Greenland. The water/ice of the Iceberg was therefore entirely fresh water, but scattered within the ice were numerous rocks and grit, some quite large.

Scientists now believe that Iceberg was first formed in Greenland thousands of years prior before hitting the Titanic, maybe as far back as 100,000 years. Yes, 100,000 years ago, when humans were still living in caves and none had even contemplated traversing the Atlantic Ocean. This is not to say that the Iceberg was floating around the Atlantic Ocean for thousands of years, but only that its snow and ice was that old. Once it broke off from the glacier of Greenland and began to head south, it did so at a rate of between a half mile per hour and three miles per hour. So it may have been in the water for a few years before it met the Titanic.

And this was no tiny iceberg.

It is believed that the Iceberg was about 400 feet long and weighed around one and half metric tons. When you consider that 90% of icebergs are actually underwater, the Iceberg was truly a massive edifice.

And this was a tough iceberg.

In addition to the rocks and grit that partially comprised the Iceberg, North Atlantic iceberg ice tends to be very hard and strong. Although only about 10% as hard as concrete, iceberg ice is still much harder than an average ice cube and when combined with the rocks and grit they are capable of generating hundreds of tons of force if smashed against a ship's hull.

And size does matter when it comes to the destructive force of icebergs.

Ignored Warnings

For historians, one of the most unfortunate results of the Titanic tragedy was that most of the crew and captain went down with the ship. There is no recording of any type that can tell us what the captain and his crew may have tried to do just before and after the Titanic hit the Iceberg.

So we are left to fill in some blanks ourselves based on what Captain Smith and his crew did.

All evidence points toward the captain being a somewhat stubborn and difficult man to deal with. We already know that he was getting old and his reflexes probably weren't what they used to be, or should be; but what happened next shows that either his hubris adversely affected his decision making, or he was losing his mental sharpness along with his reflexes.

As the Titanic entered Iceberg Alley, Captain Smith was warned via the ship's wireless system that there was an excessive amount of icebergs in the vicinity. Generally speaking, during that era, when captains received this type of news they simply slowed their ships down. Well, it is certainly common sense to move slower in low visibility, especially when you are surrounded by icebergs.

But Captain Smith wasn't following common sense!

Although Smith ordered the Titanic to take a slightly new course to the south, he maintained the ship's speed. Slowing the Titanic down just a couple of knots would've delayed the ship's arrival in New York by a couple of days or more, but apparently Smith wasn't willing to do that. They were so close, just off the coast of Nova Scotia.

Captain Smith wasn't about to let some silly icebergs steal his glory. He would arrive on time in New York, no matter what—full steam ahead!

The Iceberg is Spotted

Not long after Captain Smith ignored the warnings, fate stepped in and dealt him and the Titanic a losing hand. The Iceberg stood poised in water, barely moving, but at the Titanic's speed it would be nearly impossible to avoid. Things happened very quickly from that point on, too quick for a sixty-one-year-old ship's captain with a spotty record.

Smith had retired for the night so the command of the bridge was under First Officer William Murdoch. Two lookouts, Frederick Fleet and Reginald Lee, were also on duty looking for icebergs. The Iceberg was spotted just before 11:40 pm on April 14 at about a distance of 640 yards. You're probably thinking that at more than a football field it was surely far enough for the ship to swerve to avoid, right?

Almost immediately after spotting the Iceberg, Murdoch tried to make a sharp 21 degree portside (left) turn and almost succeeded, but just the side of the Titanic was just grazed.

It was enough of a graze to sink the ship.

After the Titanic was damaged, a series of mishaps followed, some Smith's mistakes while others were out of his control. He was, though, responsible for a lack of leadership for that point forward. Smith showed no sense of urgency, believing that the damage to the Titanic was minimal. Even when it became painfully apparent that ship was sinking, Smith took his time ordering the muster of the passengers topside because he apparently thought it would take much longer for the ship to sink.

Because of all of this, Captain Smith, in many people's minds, is blamed for many of the deaths in the Titanic tragedy.

The Lethal Gash?

An examination of the damage the Iceberg caused to the Titanic reveals that it exposed some design flaws in the ship's construction. It was originally thought that the lethal hole was a large gash more than 300 feet long, but modern ultrasounds have revealed that the gash was actually a series of small gashes that followed the plates on the hull perfectly for about twelve feet, which was enough to doom the Titanic. What was once thought to be a long, lethal gash was actually a much smaller separation in the ship's seams.

Remember, the Titanic could handle four flooded compartments, but anything more would lead to a lethal chain reaction.

As compartment after compartment began to fill with water, the Titanic's prow started to quickly sink into the ocean.

Most of the passengers felt little after the initial collision because many were asleep in their cabins, but the ones who were awake didn't feel much either. It was a glancing blow and due to the immense size of the Titanic it felt like little more than a bump in the road.

Within about fifteen minutes, though, anyone awake would have felt off with their balance and by midnight it would've been apparent that something was wrong.

Captain Smith finally ordered the mustering of the passengers topside at 12:05 am.

Modern maritime experts have examined Titanic's collision and most have determined that she would've been better off with a direct hit on the Iceberg. The Titanic's sister ship, Olympic, later survived a direct hit from a destroyer and was able to limp back into port. Also, other ships have survived direct hits on icebergs in the years after the Titanic disaster. If the Titanic would've hit the Iceberg head on, it would have sustained damage to its prow, but would've been able to safely make it to Halifax.

But for Murdoch, it was one of those fateful choices that had fatal repercussions for thousands of people.

It's All Greek

After the mustering of the passengers was ordered, there was no immediate rush, which was not helped by the captain's ineffective leadership. We'll get back to him in a minute. The first-class passengers only had a short distance to go to the lifeboats, but it was different story down below in third-class. Contrary to some fictional accounts and that have been spread over the last 100 years, the third-class passengers weren't locked in by the gates.

If you remember, the gates were only waist high and guarded by attendants.

The third-class passengers were included in the general mustering alarm and ordered topside, but there were of course things working against their survival. Their cabins were the farthest from the top deck so they therefore theoretically would've got there after everyone else.

But there was no sense of urgency immediately after the mustering was ordered, even among the third-class passengers.

Almost, if not more, problematic for the third-class passengers was their lack of homogeneity.

There is another misplaced idea about the third-class passengers that they were all the same type of poor, desperate people. The reality is that although the third-class passengers may have been poor compared to the first-class passengers, if you remember, a third-class ticket on board the Titanic was not a cheap seat. And the third-class passengers were quite diverse in terms of their incomes, professions, and educations.

As well as their countries of origin.

Although English was the most commonly spoken language in third-class, a good share also spoke German, different Scandinavian languages, Italian, Russian, Polish, and a scattering of Middle Eastern Christians on board spoke Arabic. Oh yeah, there were also some speaking Greek. When it became apparent that ship was going down and the mad rush for the lifeboats ensued, the variety of languages made the situation more chaotic.

And fatal for some of the third-class passengers who couldn't communicate with the English speaking crew.

A Lack of Leadership

After Captain Smith ordered the mustering of the passengers to the top deck, he did little else of value for his ship, crew, or passengers. Although the captain had recently had problems on the high seas, this was the first tragedy he faced and by all accounts he performed poorly in the face of adversity.

It wasn't until after 1 am that all of his bridge officers even knew that the ship was sinking and he failed to properly order the crew to put passengers in the lifeboats. When the crew finally did start putting passengers in the lifeboats it was as if they didn't know what they were doing, putting too few passengers in some and overloading others.

Captain Smith was also at least partially to blame for this.

While the crew was in Southampton awaiting the passengers, they received minimal training on proper lifeboat and evacuation techniques, having only done one drill. The crew was scheduled to do one more lifeboat drill before leaving Southampton but Smith cancelled it.

As the lifeboats were about to be loaded with passengers, it was reported that Captain Smith stood on the deck starring into the ocean. Second Officer Charles Lightoller recalled, "I yelled at the top of my voice, 'Hadn't we better get the women and children into the boats, sir?' He heard me and nodded reply."

Captain Smith would indeed go down with his ship, but it was little consolation to the loved ones of those who perished.

The Lifeboats

In fairness to Captain Smith, not everything that went wrong during the Titanic disaster was his fault. Harland and Wolff and the White Star Line never dreamed that such a major tragedy would happen to their premier ship so they were underprepared. This was perhaps most apparent with the lifeboats.

The Titanic only had twenty lifeboats that could carry about 1,200 people, which was just over half of the passengers and crew on the ship. The lifeboats consisted of thirty "clinker" type boats that were thirty feet long and nine feet wide. They were equipped with ten oars, a sail, and some food and water. There were also two small cutters, and four collapsible lifeboats that were twenty-seven feet long and five feet wide.

Now you are probably thinking, "Why didn't either Harland and Wolff or the White Star Line equip the Titanic with more lifeboat?"

This is definitely a legitimate question and one that was asked repeatedly in the months and years after the tragedy. In fairness to Harland and Wolff and the White Star Line, they were just following policies of other ocean liners at the time by having fewer lifeboats on hand that could accommodate everyone. Although ship accidents were not common, they were also not necessarily uncommon, but tragedies the size of the Titanic's sinking were almost unheard of. So Harland and Wolff built the Titanic, and all of their ocean liners for that matter, with that in mind. The lifeboats were never intended to "save" all of the ships passengers indefinitely, but to ferry them to a rescue ship.

If you remember, the North Atlantic was being traversed by numerous other ocean liners as well as cargo ships. This was before the first flight across the Atlantic so air cargo and travel was still a few decades in the future. The fact that all ships had wireless communication also meant, theoretically, that one of those ships could be reached almost instantaneously and then reach the damaged ship fairly quickly.

Of course, having less lifeboats on hand saved money and safety regulations were not what they are today so there was nothing keeping Harland and Wolff from only installing twenty lifeboats.

Once the lifeboats began being dropped into the ocean, the lack of training by the crew and the lack of leadership from the captain only aggravated the already desperate situation.

Lifeboat Number 1

Launching the lifeboats proved to be a true fiasco that unnecessarily cost the lives of many people. The boats were launched much later than they should've been and when they were everything was done in an unorganized, hectic manner—some lifeboats were overloaded while others had well below their capacity.

When the evacuations began, the general rule was women and children first, with the first-class passengers getting first dibs just by nature of their proximity to the lifeboats. Due to the extremely feminine nature of women in Edwardian society at the time, though, at least a couple of men were sent with each of the early lifeboats to row.

But when panic sets in, plans often fall apart.

Lifeboat number 1 was one of the cutters located on the side of the Titanic. It was actually the fourth lifeboat launched from the Titanic just after 1 am, but didn't hit the water for another ten minutes after it was hung up on its descent.

Lifeboat number 1 had a capacity of forty, but only twelve were on board and most of them were men. It was filled with a combination of crew and elite from both sides of the Atlantic, including American businessman Charles Stengel and British noble Cosmo Duff-Gordon and his wife Lucy. The only women on the boat were Lucy and her secretary.

The Duff-Gordons faced accusations of misconduct in the months and years after the disaster over what are for the most part unsubstantiated rumors. One allegation was that Cosmo pushed ignored the women and children and pushed his way onto the boat. But of course, he wasn't the only man on that boat. The other accusation is that he bribed the crew rowing the boat to ignore survivors floating in the sea.

Neither of those accusations were ever proven but it didn't stop people from repeating them for the rest of Cosmo's life. Cosmo and Lucy are also often depicted as cold, uncaring snobs in many fictional retellings of the Titanic disaster.

I guess wealthy British men always make for a good bad guy, right?

CQD

Just after midnight, at about the same time the passengers were mustered to the top deck, Captain Smith began sending distress calls. Jack Phillips and Harold Bride, the Marconi Company radio operators, began furiously typing out the letter "CQD." Although most took CQD to mean "Come quick danger," the CQ was actually for a general call, while D stood for distress. It was more accurately translated as "All stations, distress."

The two wireless operators were swamped with a backlog of messages that night and Phillips failed to message to the bridge about the particular iceberg field the Titanic encountered. To be fair to Phillips, the officers probably would've ignored the warnings anyway.

Bride, who was working as the two men worked in shifts, woke to the unraveling disaster. He told Phillips to send another distress under the new sign "SOS." By 2 am the wireless room was inoperable and the men were relieved of command. Phillips had to fight another crew member for his lifejacket as he attempted to abandon ship.

Phillips and Bride then split up. One of the two wireless operators was fortunate enough to survive.

The SS *Californian*

About fifteen miles away on the other side of the iceberg field the Titanic wandered into was the British steamship *Californian*. The Californian was primarily a transport ship, specializing in bringing American cotton back to the United Kingdom. On the night of April 14 and morning of April 15, 1912, she was empty beside her crew and was on her way back to America, piloted by Captain Stanley Lord.

Lord was criticized heavily in the months and years after the Titanic disaster for not doing more, but the reality is that he did try to help and once the ship started sinking there was little he could do.

The Californian's wireless operators sent several warnings to the Titanic about large icebergs between the two ships in the two hours before the collision, but Phillips ignored the messages. As we discussed earlier, Phillips had a back log of messages he was working on and he was also in contact with the relay station in Cape Race, Newfoundland. The Californian sent a final warning at 10:30 pm, which Phillips responded to be messaging "Shut up! Shut up! I'm working Cape Race."

The Californian wireless operators honored Phillips' request.

By the time the Titanic hit the Iceberg and started sending distress signals, the Californian had its wireless receiver turned off for the night for some reason.

Still, the lookouts on the Titanic could clearly see the Californian and tried to signal it. They figured that it was only five or so miles away.

Actually, the Californian was about eighteen miles away and it was on the other side of the iceberg field, so it may as well have been in another world. Before radar was a reality, mariners had to rely on their own eyes and whatever tools aided them, such as binoculars and telescopes. Good mariners knew to take the curvature of the globe into consideration, but apparently in the panic of the sinking ship the Titanic crew didn't consider super refraction when they tried to signal the Californian.

They would have to look elsewhere for help.

Father Thomas Byles

The Titanic had several heroes in its final hours. There were those who gave up their seats for others, some of whom we've already mentioned. And as we will see later, there were those who rescued the survivors from the icy sea.

Then there was Thomas Byles.

Father Thomas Byles was a forty-two-year-old Roman Catholic priest who was dedicated to the Church and helping others. Born into an English Protestant family, Byles converted to Catholicism while studying theology at Oxford and then studied for the priesthood in Rome. He was on his way to officiate his brother William's wedding in New York when tragedy struck.

Byles purchased a second-class ticket and since most of the first-class blue bloods were Protestants, he spent most of his time with his fellow second-class passengers. When the Titanic hit the Iceberg, Byles was on the top deck, which allowed him to help other passengers into lifeboats, while denying a spot for himself.

When the ship finally sank, Byles was with more than a hundred passengers in the stern. He reportedly heard their confessions and gave them absolution before they all perished together beneath the icy waters.

Byles had originally planned to make the voyage on another ship, but changed his ticket to the Titanic at the last moment. The circumstances surrounding Father Byles' departure and his actions during the disaster made many think that divine providence had a hand in things. Pope Pius X agreed by declaring that Byles was a martyr for the Church.

There have also recently been efforts within the Church to make Father Thomas Byles a saint.

Meanwhile, Down Below

When boiler room number 4 began being flooded around 1:20 am the engineers, electricians, and firemen could've abandoned their posts. By that time many of the crew members were beginning to leave their posts and some had even evacuated the ship.

But the crew in the bowels of the ship knew that if there was even a slight chance of saving the ship they had to do what they could. They also knew that even if the ship couldn't be saved, it was important to keep the electricity on so that distress calls could continue to be sent on the wireless.

The postal clerks also continued to work to save the mail!

Yes, it seems strange that they would do so. Perhaps like many they weren't aware of the gravity of the situation until it was too late. Or maybe they really believed in what they were doing that much. Either way, all of the postmen men along with all thirty-five of the Titanic's engineers and electricians perished in the lower decks of the ship.

Isidor and Ida Strauss

Even before the last lifeboat was launched around 2:05 am, many of the Titanic passengers had become consigned to their fates. We already know about the second and third-class passengers praying with Father Byles, but there were also a number of other passengers in all classes who simply didn't want to leave a loved one behind.

One of these people was Ida Strauss.

Ida Strauss was the wife of former United States Congressman and co-owner of Macy's department store, Isidor Strauss. Isidor and Ida were returning from the winter in the south of France when disaster struck on the Titanic. It was reported later that the relatively elderly Isidor—he was sixty-seven and she was sixty-three—was offered a seat in a lifeboat with his wife, but he refused until every woman and child was seated.

Ida then gave her seat to another woman and said to her husband, "We have been living together for many years. Where you go, I go."

The couple was last seen alive sitting on the top deck in deck chairs.

There were so many other cases like the Strauss's, where small acts of bravery were done be people stoically facing the end of their lives.

The Rockets' Red Glare

At about 12:30 am the crew began firing rockets as distress beacons. Crew members apparently fired several rockets from two different stations on the ship—one from the port side and one from the starboard side. Although crew members of the Californian later claimed to have seen eight rockets in the sky, they were all but worthless.

Once again, Captain Smith failed to effectively lead his crew.

Distress rockets, which were essentially giant flares, were used during the period as a last resort to alert other ships that something was wrong. The rockets would be fired in a very specific sequence of one minute intervals to tell other ships what the problem was and the location.

The Titanic crew fired their rockets randomly.

The crew fired the rockets for about forty minutes until they were gone. Since the rockets weren't fired in the proper intervals, the Californian crew thought nothing of it. It probably wouldn't have mattered much anyway because there was that big iceberg field between them.

Random Facts

1. The Grand Banks off Nova Scotia, which is where the Titanic sank, was once a prime commercial fishing location. Due to overfishing, though, the Canadian government had to ban certain types of fishing.
2. It is believed that the Titanic received six iceberg warnings on April 14.
3. Fleet and Lee were seated in the ship's crow's nest, about ninety-five feet above the deck, when they spotted the Iceberg.
4. Fleet was the lookout who spotted the Iceberg. He rang the bell, telephoned the bridge, and exclaimed "iceberg, right ahead."
5. Although many believe that Captain Smith was at least partially responsible for the disaster, a statue was erected in in memory, which stands in Lichfield, England.
6. William Byles and his fiancé Katherine didn't cancel their wedding. They had another priest perform the ceremony and immediately after changed from their wedding clothes into mourning clothes.
7. Water rushed into the Titanic's hull at the rate of seven long tons per second, which was far greater than the ship's pumping system could handle.
8. The term for when a ship is tilting is "listing."
9. Andrews and the Guarantee Group were immediately notified of the damage by the captain.
10. Andrews was last seen assisting passengers evacuate the ship. History has been kind to his memory, as he has been depicted as a hero in both historical studies and nearly every fictional account.
11. There were more than 400,000 items of mail on the Titanic when it sank.
12. Lifeboat number 7 was the first lifeboat launched. It only had twenty-eight people in the sixty-five person capacity boat.
13. Collapsible boat D from the port side was the last lifeboat successfully launched. It was launched just after 2 am with about thirty-seven people out of forty-seven seats.

14.   At 2:21 am, as Collapsible boat B was about to launch, a rush of water onto the Titanic flipped the lifeboat over. Some passengers survived by clinging to its hull.

15.   Collapsible boat A was also washed away and filled with water, although about a dozen people crawled into it for survival.

16.   There was a report that just after midnight, some passengers on the top deck were playing soccer with ice chunks from the collision.

17.   Although the "SOS" distress call was fairly new when the Titanic operators sent one, contrary to rumors, it was not the first time in history one was sent.

18.   Many believe that the evacuation order stated "women and children only," but it was in fact "women and children first." The crew itself was confused about the order, which is why many of the first lifeboats had such few occupants.

19.   The Californian was sunk in 1915 during World War I by a German U-boat in the Mediterranean Sea.

20.   There were eight Chinese passengers in third-class on board the Titanic. All were sailors headed to New York for work and six of them survived.

Test Yourself – Questions and Answers

1. Which country was the SS *Californian* from?
    a. Great Britain/United Kingdom
    b. Argentina
    c. United States

2. Isidor Strauss was the co-owner of which major department store?
    a. Herod's
    b. Macey's
    c. Target

3. What was the distress signal ships used before SOS?
    a. CQD
    b. LOL
    c. OMG

4. Where did the iceberg that the Titanic hit come from?
    a. Antarctica
    b. Alaska
    c. Greenland

5. How many lifeboats were on the Titanic?
    a. 5
    b. 20
    c. 100

Answers

1. a
2. b
3. a
4. c
5. b

CHAPTER FIVE
SURVIVING AND DYING IN THE TRAGEDY

When the Titanic sank below the icy waters of the North Atlantic, many people's stories had come to an end. You've read about some of the harrowing tales and selfless acts of heroism in the final two plus hours of the Titanic, now you will read about the equally harrowing tales of the many people who survived the sinking of the ship, but had to fight the frigid waters to stay alive.

It was usually a matter of luck if a person survived.

Those who made it safely unto stable lifeboats were later picked up alive, while those who had to tread water in the icy ocean usually died. It was simple as that.

Those who did survive were certainly happy they did, but some were burdened with survivor's guilt and others suffered from post-traumatic stress disorder, long before it was even a recognized disorder.

You Didn't Want to Be a Guy in Second-Class

Once the first few lifeboats were launched and it was apparent that the Titanic was sinking fast, all decorum went out the window. The ship's crew continued to give preference to women and children, but class no longer mattered much.

And that was a situation that statistics show favored some groups over others.

The demographic that suffered the most was second-class men. Overall, 167 out of 285 second-class passengers were lost for a mortality rate of around 59%, which is expectedly lower than the third-class mortality rate of 75%, but higher than the first-class rate of 38%. Numerous factors play a role in those numbers: second-class was farther from the top deck than first-class but closer than third-class and the vast majority of second-class passengers were English speakers so they didn't have communication problems.

But a closer look at those statistics reveals that second-class *men* had a higher mortality rate than any other group on the Titanic.

Only fourteen second-class male passengers survived, or about 9%. Lawrence Beesley was one of those few men in second-class to survive, escaping on lifeboat number 13 in the second wave of evacuations.

Beesley's account was later published in book form as *The Loss of The SS Titanic: Its Story and Its Lessons, by One of the Survivors.*

In contrast, about 21% of all third-class men survived the tragedy, which of course raises the simple question: why?

When historians have been asked this question, most point toward the social backgrounds of the men. Most second-class men were middle class school teachers, academics, clergy etc., who were accustomed to following the rules and rarely having to use their physical strength. Perfect for productive members of society, but not for survival conditions.

On the other hand, the third-class men were factory workers, teamsters, farmers, and were often familiar with manual labor, and therefore physically stronger than their second-class counterparts, and many were also used to hardships and at times violence.

So when the emergency hit critical mass, the third-class men weren't afraid to push to the front of the lifeboat lines and, if need be, punch someone to get a place. While the third-class men were fighting for spots on the lifeboats, the second-class men stood by politely waiting for their turn.

You could almost argue it was a case of Darwinism in a microcosm.

J. Bruce Ismay

We already met Bruce Ismay earlier in our story, remember? He was the

English businessman and chairman of the White Star Line who was largely responsible for the Olympic class line of ships. Ismay often went on his ships' maiden voyages and as the Titanic was being built there was little doubt in his mind that he would be on the White Star Line's crown jewel's maiden voyage.

Bruce Ismay survived the Titanic disaster.

By all accounts, Ismay requited himself fairly honorably as the ship sank and took one of the last lifeboats, collapsible boat C, at 2:00 am. The boat was filled to its capacity of forty-four, but before it was launched it was rushed by a crowd of stewards and third-class passengers desperate to be saved.

The ship's purser fired a couple warning shots from a pistol to hold the crowd back.

As the boat nearly filled its capacity, a final call was made for any remaining women and children but a number of men took the final seats. Ismay was one of those men.

Once the lifeboat was safely launched, Ismay sat stoically looking forward with his back to the sinking ship, refusing to watch its final few minutes of life. After Ismay was safely on the *Carpathia*, he said and ate very little but sent a message to the White Star Line's New York office that read: "Deeply regret advise you Titanic sank this morning fifteenth after collision iceberg, resulting serious loss life further particulars later. Bruce Ismay."

What followed next was the complete destruction of Ismay's reputation by the international media that continues until today. He was called a brute and a coward and was called before government investigations to answer for his actions. Nearly every fictional account of the Titanic disaster has also portrayed Ismay as one of the bad guys.

Much of the negative attitude toward Ismay is certainly derived from the fact that he survived. In people's minds he should have went down with his creation, but the reality is that he was not the captain and was never under any obligation to do so.

He was also on one of the last lifeboats to leave and witnesses reported that he was helping a number of women and children to safety before he evacuated.

It is probably safe to say that history has unfairly treated Ismay.

The Unsinkable Molly Brown

You couldn't find many more interesting and engaging personalities on the Titanic's passenger list than American Margaret Brown. Brown was born into a poor working class family in Hannibal, Missouri in 1867 and later moved to Colorado in her early adulthood, which is where she met her future husband, James Joseph Brown.

Although Brown was also poor, he was bright, ambitious, and was the recipient of fortune when his upstart mining company hit gold. The Browns quickly became very wealthy people and in no time Margaret was hob knobbing with America's rich and powerful, like John Jacob Astor.

In late 1911 and early 1912, Margaret was traveling in Europe and Egypt when she met up with the Astors and decided to take the Titanic back with them to America.

When tragedy struck, Brown spent the first hour and a half helping other passengers to the top deck and into lifeboats. She was offered a seat on more than one lifeboat but refused. Finally, as lifeboat number 6 was being lowered into the ocean at 1:10 am, a crew member picked Brown up and dropped her into the boat. It only had twenty-nine people out of a sixty-five person capacity.

Lookout Frederick Fleet was also on lifeboat number 6.

It was while she was in the lifeboat that Margaret Brown acquired her nickname. Brown took an oar for herself and demanded that the women be allowed to row in order to stay warm. She then demanded that they row back to find survivors.

There is no historical consensus if lifeboat number 6 actually did search for survivor and if they rescued any if they did. No matter, the legend of the

"Unsinkable Molly Brown" was born. She later went on to start a Titanic relief organization, among other philanthropic groups, and was an actress in the 1920s.

She is universally portrayed positively in fictional accounts.

Children on the Titanic

Although there were a number of children on the Titanic, their stories are often neglected, probably because most were helpless, or at least perceived that way. Also, few of the children who survived the Titanic disaster went on to talk much about it in their adult lives as people would do today. It was a very different time where those affected by misfortune would rather go back to their lives than profit from tragedy.

What is considered a child has changed quite a bit over the decades, with the standard today being anyone under the age of eighteen. When the Titanic sailed, children were generally considered to be under the age of fifteen, although this was not a concrete rule and varied from country to country— few people had cars and young people often quit school and married in their teens.

There were 126 children age fourteen or younger on the Titanic, of which fifty-nine died. All but two of those children were in third-class.

Fourteen-year-old George Sweet was the only child in second-class to perish on the Titanic. He was probably stopped from entering a lifeboat due to his size. George died just one day shy of his fifteenth birthday.

The only first-class child to die was two-year-old Helen Allison. Little Helen died when she and her parents, Hudson and Bess, were separated from her brother Trevor. They continued to search for Trevor until the ship sank. Unknown to them, Trevor made it safely aboard a lifeboat with the Allison's nurse, Alice Cleaver.

Due to the number of reasons discussed earlier that made evacuation in third-class slower and less efficient, fifty-three of the seventy-six children in that section went down with the Titanic.

The Orphans of the Titanic

Among all of the children in second-class who survived were two brothers, ages two and three, known as Lola and Momon Hoffman. The Hoffman boys were traveling in second-class with their father, Louis Hoffman, at least that is what his ticket said.

But nothing seemed right about the presumably single father.

He seemed to treat his sons well and was with them at all times, but things just didn't add up. Hoffman portrayed himself as German or German-Jewish, but he was only heard speaking French, and with a Slavic accent. He claimed that he was a widower and on his way to the United States to begin a new life, but he offered few details about where he was going once he got there or what he was going to do for work.

The reality is that Louis Hoffman's name was really Michel Navratil, a Slovakian-French immigrant who spent a lot of time moving around Europe. He lived in London for a while, which is where he met an Italian woman, Marcelle Caretto, who would become his wife and the mother of his two boys, Michel Junior and Edmond, not Lola and Momon.

As a cynical citizen of the twenty-first century, you can probably guess what happened next.

Michel's and Marcelle's marriage failed and Marcelle won custody of the boys. As is the case sometimes today, both parties were not happy with the judge's ruling. Michel decided to take matters into his own hands by buying tickets on the Titanic with the idea that he and the boys would be safe in the United States.

And in 1912 he would've been right.

When disaster struck, Michel redeemed himself by fighting his way to the top deck with his boys in his arms. He made sure they were on the last lifeboat that made it, collapsible boat D. Michel Junior claims that as his father put them in the boat, he told him: "My child, when your mother comes for you, as she surely will, tell her that I loved her dearly and still do. Tell her I expected her to follow us, so that we might all live happily together in the peace and freedom of the New World."

The boys' identifies were unknown for some time so they became known as the "Titanic Orphans." Once they were identified, they were sent back to France to live with their mother.

Both boys went on to lead interesting lives. Edmond was in the French Army in World War II, but spent most of the war in a German prisoner-of-war camp. The internment gave him lasting health problems and he died in 1953 at the age of forty-three.

Michel Junior earned a PhD in philosophy and enjoyed a long career as a professor and academic. He was the last male survivor of the Titanic, dying in 2001 at the age of ninety-two.

In the Water

When the last lifeboat left, there were still about 1,500 on board the Titanic waiting to be saved. As we've already discussed, some became resigned to their fates and spent their last few moments on this earth praying or in the embrace of a loved one.

But the human instinct for survival in incredibly strong, so most of the remaining people tried to do what they could to survive.

They quickly made their way to the aft of the ship, which was at an angle of about forty-five degrees by 2:15 am. Hundreds of passengers began falling from the ship in groups and as individuals, hoping to be rescued. By 2:20 am the Titanic was submerged in the Atlantic, taking hundreds more with her.

Most of the people who fell from the ship into the water would've died almost instantly. The shock of the near freezing water would've forced a natural reaction to take a deep breath, which caused immediate drowning. Those who weren't fortunate enough to die instantly succumbed to hypothermia within thirty minutes.

Women were actually better suited for survival in the water due to having a higher percentage of body fat on average and those who tried to swim for help usually died as well. One would think that the physical activity would raise the body's temperature, but in conditions that cold it only serves to make things worse.

Only a handful of those who went into the water survived, one of which was Rhoda Abbott.

Rhoda and her boys were swept into the ocean when the Titanic finally went under. They all were holding hands until they hit the water but were separated during the impact. Rhoda swam for a while trying to find her sons, but to no avail. Finally she found the damaged collapsible boat A and crawled in with some other survivors. Most of the others died.

Rhoda Abbott suffered from severe asthma, post-traumatic stress, and survivors' guilt for the remainder of her life.

The Last One In

Charles Joughin, the Titanic's chief baker, was described as a kind and jovial man. He loved his work, got along well with the other crew members, and performed well under pressure. All of those qualities played a role when tragedy struck on April 14.

Joughin was in his bunk when the Titanic hit the Iceberg, but felt the impact and knew that something was wrong. He reported to his work station and immediately went to work supplying the lifeboats with provisions. After helping passengers into lifeboats, the boat he was supposed to pilot left without him.

So the easy going chef did what anyone would do in a similar situation—he went below deck for some drinks!

Joughin then went back up to throw life vest into the water because by then the last lifeboat had left. When the Titanic finally sank into oblivion at 2:20 am, Jouhgin rode it down from the aft, later claiming that his head never went in the water.

He was the last known survivor on the Titanic.

As if Joughin's survival tale wasn't incredible enough so far, what happened next was truly miraculous. He survived or possibly two hours in the water, which is much longer than most. The reason for Jouhgin's survival is connected to the science we discussed in the previous section. As a chef, Joughin liked to sample his food so he had a bit of extra fat on his body, which gave him insulation from the frigid temperatures.

He finally came across the overturned collapsible lifeboat B and crawled on until he was rescued. While Joughin tried to survive on top of the lifeboat he met wireless operator Harold Bride.

Harold Bride

You'll remember from the last chapter that Harold Bride was one of the two Titanic wireless operators along with Jack Phillips. You'll also remember that the two men stayed at their posts almost until the very end and that things got pretty dicey for them on their way out.

Phillips didn't make it.

Bride made it up top and along with some other crew members was attempting to launch collapsible lifeboat B when it was washed off the deck upside down.

Bride was underneath the lifeboat when it went out to sea!

The quick thinking Bride remained calm, though, and remained with the boat for a while, surviving on the air from the air pocket. Once he was sure that the boat was clear of the Titanic, Bride swam underneath to the outside and climbed on the hull. He was later joined by Charles Joughin, Jack Thayer, Archibald Gracie, and others.

One by one survivors kept falling off the boat during the early morning hours due to exhaustion and exposure. Finally, when rescue boats arrived hours later Bride, Joughin, Thayer, Gracie, and about twenty-six other men were still alive on the overturned boat.

Puppies and Kitties on the Titanic

There is no doubt that those of us who are animal lovers certainly love our cats and dogs. Life just wouldn't be the same without our furry little buddies, which was just as true for people more than 100 years ago than it is today. So because of people's affections for their pets, there were plenty of cuddly critters on board the Titanic.

Although the exact number is not known, it is estimated that there were around twelve dogs that were traveling with their masters. Rich women carrying lap dogs as if they were fashion accessories was not an uncommon sight on the decks of the Titanic.

Nearly all of these women were American blue bloods traveling in first-class. And you can probably just about imagine what it would've been like to interact with one of these women!

Passengers were allowed to keep lap dogs in their cabins, but most dogs were housed below in deck F.

Keeping with maritime traditions of the period, the Titanic had a feline mascot named Jenny that had just given birth to a litter of kittens before leaving Southampton. Jenny and her kittens were well-fed, living on a combination of scraps from the kitchen and an occasional rat or mouse mama killed in one of her ship wide hunts.

Because mariners tend to be on the superstitious side, Jenny and her kittens were treated quite well by the crew and allowed free in the area around the galley.

Unfortunately, Jenny and her brood didn't survive.

Only three dogs survived the disaster, one of which belong to the heiress Elizabeth Rothschild, who refused to board lifeboat number 6 without her dog.

Losing "Face"

Few of the survivors suffered more attacks on their reputations than Bruce Ismay, with the possible exception of Masabumi Hosono.

Apart from being the only Japanese passenger on board the Titanic, Hosono was not unlike most of his fellow second-class passengers. The forty-two-year-old had built a nice middle-class career for himself in the rapidly modernizing Japan of the early twentieth century. He worked for the Ministry of Transportation and was fluent in Russian, which is how he ended up on the Titanic. After conducting research on the Russian rail system for the Japanese government, Hosono traveled through Europe and caught the Titanic. He was then to travel through the United States and finally catch another ship in San Francisco back to Japan.

For the most part, Hosono was a quiet, efficient civil servant who longed to return to his wife and children in Japan.

When the evacuations began, Hosono was at first held back because the crew thought he was a Chinese passenger in third-class. After making his way through the crowd, Hosono found a place on lifeboat number 10 at 1:50 am.

Although news traveled slowly 100 years ago, transportation was even slower. By the time Hosono finally made it to San Francisco for the final leg of his journey home, newspapers in the United States and Japan had reported about the Japanese passenger who had survived the Titanic.

Most of those reports were not good and many were untrue.

Some reports untruly stated that Hosono dressed like a woman to get on a lifeboat and was described as a "stowaway" on the lifeboat by survivor Archibald Gracie. The rumors cause Hosono to temporarily lose his job and face. Although he later got his job back, he lived in shame for the rest of his life, which was then tragically passed on to his ancestors.

Only recently has Masabumi Hosono's reputation been salvaged.

Dying in the Lifeboats

When the last of the lightboats were launched, dozens of men made final, desperate attempts to save their lives by trying to jump from the ship into the boats. Some of the men landed safely in the lifeboats, while others landed in the water near the boats. A handful were lucky enough to be picked up by the lifeboats, but only the ones who were immediately scooped up usually survived and even some of them died.

Lifeboat number 4 was the last wooden lifeboat to be launched at 1:50 am. After it was lowered into the water, the crew member in charge of rowing, Quartermaster Walter Perkis, ordered the boat to pick up survivors in the water.

The lifeboat picked up a handful of men treading water, but it was too later for two crew members who died of hyperthermia—steward Sidney Siebert and seaman William Lyons.

American William Fisher Hoyt was another man who was pulled from the water a bit too late.

The self-made Hoyt had been in Europe on business and was traveling back to the United States on a first-class ticket on the Titanic. He was on the Titanic until the very end, suffering a head injury when the ship sank.

Hoyt was spotted by Fifth Officer Harold Lowe, who was commanding lifeboat number 14 and ordered it back to search for survivors. The occupants of lifeboat number 14 had a tough time pulling the portly Hoyt from the water. The men in the lifeboat tried to take care of Hoyt, but as Lowe later said, "He was too far gone when we picked him up."

By 2:30 am the pleading cries and screams from those in the water were gone, but many of the survivors who heard them would be haunted by those sounds for the rest of their lives.

The Youngest Survivor

Michel Navratil was the last male survivor of the Titanic, but Millvina Dean was the last official overall survivor. Millvina was born on February 2, 1912, so when she boarded the Titanic with her parents, Bertram Frank and Georgette, and nearly two-year-old brother, Bertram Vere she was only two-months-old. Bertram Frank planned to move his family to Kansas where he planned to run a tobacco shop with some family members.

When the Titanic hit the Iceberg, Bertram Frank was awake and knew that something was wrong. He quickly gathered his family and brought them to the top deck. Betram's quick thinking ensured that his family were among the first of the third-class passengers to successfully evacuate the ship. Millvina, Georgette, and Bertram Vere were place on lifeboat number 10 and whisked away to safety.

Bertram Frank perished along with the Titanic.

Georgette lived with Millvina and Betram Vere in the United States, but the stress of being a single mother in that time was too much so she returned to England where she had family support.

Millvina would lead a full and interesting life, but no matter what she did the specter of the Titanic disaster and the fact that she was its youngest survivor seemed to play a role in everything she did. It was probably fitting that the youngest survivor would also last all other survivors. On May 31, 2009, Millvina Dean died of pneumonia a the age of ninety-seven.

Her ashes were scattered in the Southampton harbor.

Second Officer Lightoller

We've already met Second Officer Charles Lightoller earlier in our story as he played an important role in all phases of the Titanic disaster. He led an exciting, interesting, and important life before and after the Titanic, but it was his actions on the Titanic that made him famous.

Charles Lightoller was born in 1874 in a small town in northern England. Rather than go to work in a mine or factory, he chose a career on the high seas at the young age of thirteen. He eventually found work with the White

Star Line, sailing under Captain Smith and working his way up the ranks.

By the time Lightoller was promoted to First Officer on the Titanic, he was still a relatively young thirty-eight, but an experienced old sea dog in many ways.

But like his captain, Lightoller made some mistakes along the way.

One of the first and probably most fatal mistakes Lightoller made was interpreting Captain Smith's "women and children first" evacuation order as "women and children only." Because of this, Lightoller often sent lifeboats out at half capacity or less. For example, when he found lifeboat number 2 occupied primarily by men he pulled out his revolver and said, "Get out of there, you damned cowards! I'd like to see every one of you overboard!"

Lifeboat number 2 was then launched and under half capacity.

In fairness to Lightoller, though, he never attempted to leave in one of the lifeboats when he clearly could have.

As the Titanic began its final descent into the water and water began rushing over the deck, Lightoller tried to launch collapsible lifeboat B but it flipped over and he was unable to do so. When it was evident that the Titanic would sink at any moment, Lightroller dove into the water to prevent from being sucked under from the force of the sinking ship.

But he was sucked under anyway.

After struggling to free himself from a grate that he was caught on, a blast of warm water from a vent. He was sucked under once more but was finally able to reach the surface, where by coincidence he found the overturned collapsible boat B.

There he met Harold Bride and the men latter fished Charles Joughin from the water.

Lightoller organized the men on the boat to properly distribute their weight, thereby preventing more deaths.

He was the highest ranking officer to survive the Titanic disaster, which combined with his initial handling of the evacuation led to some criticism, but his actions on collapsible boat B pretty much saved his reputation.

Lightoller later served in World War I and piloted a rescue boat during the Dunkirk evacuation of World War II. He died at the age of seventy-eight during the Great Smog of 1952 in London.

The Countess of Rothes

The movers and shakers in Titanic's first-class cabins included a number of members of European nobility, one of which was Noël Leslie, the Countess of Rothes. Although Noël Dyer-Edwards was born into money, she married into the aristocracy when she married Norman Leslie, the 19th Earl of Rothes in 1900.

The couple owned homes in England and Scotland, but spent most of their time in the Scottish countryside.

The attractive Noël led many charity and philanthropic efforts, helping the poor and homeless of the British Isles, as well as soldiers and veterans later in her life. Much of her time was spent donating her time and money to various organizations, but when she wasn't involved with some type of worthy cause she enjoyed traveling.

Which is what brought her to the Titanic.

The Countess and her cousin, Gladys Cherry, planned to take the Titanic to New York where they would then begin a trip across the United States and Canada, eventually uniting with Lord Rothes. The women bought a ticket for a standard first-class cabin and spent most of their time on board with each other.

When disaster struck, the Countess and Gladys were able to get seats on lifeboat number 8. While they were on the lifeboat, the Countess did a fair share of the rowing and steering, making her one of the few woman to do so during the tragedy. After they were rescued and onboard the SS *Carpathia* the Countess spent much of her time consoling and helping the third-class survivors.

No doubt owing at least partially to her good looks, charm, and high standing in society, the Countess became a media sensation in the years after the disaster and was proclaimed one of the tragedy's heroines.

The Countess was never comfortable with the title and was quick to give credit to others, such as crewman Thomas Jones, who was in charge of lifeboat number 8.

The SS *Carpathia*

After the Titanic's survivors who were fortunate enough to make it into lifeboats watched as the "ship that would never sink," sank into the icy water of the North Atlantic a plethora of intense emotions washed over them. First, they were full of dread and terror watching the ship take so many lives. Then the dread was replaced with a certain amount of relief in the knowledge that they had survived, but that in turn became guilt for those who left loved ones behind or who didn't know the status of their loved ones.

Finally, desperation and despair took over as they floated in their lifeboats, some barely clinging to life, waiting for help to arrive.

And they waited and waited!

Like the Titanic, the Carpathia was a British flagged passenger ocean liner, but it was operated by the Cunard. On April 14 the Carpathia was en route from New York to the Mediterranean Sea when it received the Titanic's distress signal via the wireless that it had hit the Iceberg and needed help.

Captain Arthur Rostron sent a message to the Titanic that the Carpathia was on its way. The Carpathia made it to the ice field around the time the Titanic sank and it took another hour and a half of careful maneuvering to make to the survivors.

Rescue operations continued until 9:00 am when the last of Titanic's lifeboats and its 705 survivors was finally on board the Carpathia. The survivors were housed in the ship's dining rooms, fed, and given medical attention. Rostron then conferred with Ismay with the men deciding that it was best to go back to New York.

The Carpathia's passengers never complained about the drastic change to their travel plans and in fact helped out wherever and however they could. There was truly a feeling of comradery and selflessness on the Carpathia.

Captain Rostron and the Carpathia crew were given commendations for their efforts to help the Titanic survivors. The Carpathia, though, was not so lucky as she was sank during World War I by a German U-boat.

Random Facts

1. Michael Navratil's body was recovered and identified by the name he bought his ticket under, "Louis Hoffman." Since no one came forward to claim the body and since the White Star Line believed he was Jewish due to the surname, Navratil was buried in a Jewish cemetery outside Halifax, Nova Scotia.
2. The facts surrounding Molly Brown's survival on the Titanic became so legendary, or sensationalized, that they were turned into a play *The Unsinkable Molly Brown* and then a 1964 film of the same name with Debbie Reynolds in the lead role. Kathy Bates perhaps most memorably played her in James Cameron's 1997 *Titanic*, capturing her humble, working-class background.
3. The destruction of Ismay's reputation began at the hands of American media magnet, William Randolph Hearst. In newspapers own by Hearst, Ismay was often referred to as "J. Brute Ismay." His reputation never recovered.
4. Archibald Butt (1865-1912) was among the elite Americans who died on the Titanic. He was a military aide to presidents Theodore Roosevelt and William Taft. More than one account stated that Butt restored order on the top deck during the evacuation as the captain stood by.
5. Millvina Dean never married nor had children.
6. Besides the puppies and kitties, there were a number of different types of birds on board the Titanic. All pets, even the birds, were required to have tickets.
7. Despite some obvious issues with the wireless operation on April 14 and 15, wireless operator Bride was considered one Titanic's heroes when he arrived in New York on the Carpathia. He gave *The New York Times* a $1,000 exclusive interview, which was a considerable sum in 1912.
8. The Titanic's lifeboats were the only pieces of the ship to be saved from the disaster. They were brought to New York along with the Carpathia, but then mysteriously disappeared. It was believed that some, or parts of them would've turned up somewhere in the world by now, but they remain missing.

9. Charles Joughin's father owned a pub so he was around the hospitality industry from a young age. He began working on ships at the young age of eleven!

10.   The Titanic's fourteen clinker-built lifeboats, which were the numbered lifeboats, were fairly well-equipped for disaster. Each had ten oars, two forty-five gallon jugs of fresh water, a lantern, and a water tight compartment that contained cookies.

11.   The Carpathia was a single funnel liner that was built primarily to transport third-class passengers. Although it had a capacity of over 2,000 passengers after it was expanded it 1905, it was only just over 500 feet long, far less than the Titanic. It was basically a case of shoving the third-class passengers into the steerage like sardines!

12.   Joseph Laroche is the only black man on the Titanic. The twenty-six-year-old engineer was on his way back to his native Haiti when disaster struck. He died but his family survived.

13.   Harold Bride continued to work for the Marconi wireless company after the disaster, but eventually married, settled in Scotland, and worked as a salesman for the latter part of his working life.

14.   There were later reports that a Newfoundland dog named Rigel rescued a number of survivors of the Titanic. Scholars doubt the story, which may have come from a combination of the geographic area near where the Titanic sank and people's general love of dogs.

15.   Passengers on ships that passed near the Titanic reported seeing bodies still floating in the area. Only the bodies of 228 people of the 1,500 were recovered, most still wearing lifejackets.

16.   The CS *Mackay-Bennett* (cable repair ship) was contracted by the White Star Line as the first vessel to recover the bodies of Titanic victims.

17.   The recovered bodies of first and second-class victims were usually embalmed and the family members were contacted. Third-class victims were usually buried at sea. The reason for the difference in treatment was more a matter of economics and less about class hatred: the families of first and

second-class passengers could usually be located and could pay for the transportation of the bodies, while the same was not so for third-class passengers.

18.   The details on the Chinese survivors is a bit sketchy. It is believed that they hid on the lifeboats until they were rescued by the Carpathia. They were then put in chains and later denied entry into the United States. Their fates are unknown.

19.   In another Titanic-Lusitania coincidence, Captain Rostron of the Carpathia later commanded the Lusitania, but lucky for him he was at the helm of another ship during World War I.

20.   Rhoda Abott remarried after the Titanic disaster and moved to Jacksonville, Florida for several years. She later moved back to England, which is where she died in 1946 at the age of seventy-three.

Test Yourself – Questions and Answers

1) Which of these animals was *not* on the Titanic?

      a. Dog
      b. Bird
      c. Cobra

2) What was the name of the ship that rescued the Titanic's survivors?

      a. Carpathia
      b. Lusitania
      c. California

3) Molly Brown's husband, James, made his money in?

      a. Oil

      b. Gold
      c. Silver

4) The only Asian passenger not in third-class was from?

      a. China

      b. Philippines
      c. Japan

5) The Second Officer of the Titanic was?

      a. James Lightoller

      b. William Riker
      c. Willie McBride

Answers

1. c
2. a
3. b
4. c
 5. b

CHAPTER SIX
THE LEGACY OF THE TITANIC

We've come a long way in our study of the Titanic. You're now familiar with how the idea of steamships and trans-Atlantic ocean travel became a reality and how that led to the construction of the Titanic. We've also looked at some of the interesting personalities who took that fateful voyage and some who died and others who lived.

We've explored how the Titanic was built and some of the reasons why it ended up on the bottom of the ocean.

Now we'll take a look at how that incredible disaster affected the course of world history, and continues to do so until today in many ways.

The Titanic disaster led to government hearings and lawsuits, sometimes ruining the reputations of those involved.

Many would say it also played a large role in the demise of the White Star Line.

We will also take a look at how the captivating stories of the Titanic has been retold in countless television shows, films, and books in fictional accounts, while at the same time the disaster has garnered a fair amount of academic interest in the final 100 years, culminating with the ship's rediscovery.

Truly, the Titanic and the lives lost in the disaster of its sinking will continue to enthrall people for decades to come.

Senator William Alden Smith

Like all politicians who reach the highest ranks of their profession, Michigan Republican Senator William Alden Smith (1859-1932) was an ambitious man who was always looking for a way to forward his career. Smith was smart, able, and developed plenty of important connections, first in Michigan and later in later in Washington, D.C.

He was also a politician who was well-versed in the adage, "never let a good crisis go to waste."

When the Titanic disaster happened, he was immediately on it.

As soon as the disaster became known, Smith immediately began organizing an inquiry into the disaster. The inquiry was conducted by a subcommittee of the Commerce Committee, which was chaired by Smith and comprised of six other Senators from around the country, three Republicans and three Democrats. The hearings were held from April 19, 1912 to May 25, 1912 in New York and Washington, with the New York proceedings held at John Jacob Astor's Waldorf-Astoria Hotel.

More than eighty witnesses were called to testify, including Charles, Lightoller, Harold Bride, and Arthur Rostron.

The committee concluded several different things, but foremost was essentially that Captain Smith was incompetent.

The committee's final report led to some changes in maritime practices, but not everyone was happy.

Especially in Britain.

In fairness to the British, it did seem that Senator Smith was guilty of a fair amount of grandstanding, no doubt to further his career, but their criticism of the proceedings was based on a fair amount of nationalism.

You see, the British were at the tail end of their empire, but they still had the largest empire in the world and didn't particularly like being upstaged, especially by the Yanks!

Although Smith demonstrated a lack of maritime knowledge during the hearings and was at times overly aggressive, the British press was unrelenting, portraying him as a rube, a redneck, and a backwoods hillbilly. There was simply no way that the British would allow the Yanks, especially one as uncouth as Senator Smith, to have the last say on the Titanic.

The British would conduct their own hearings.

John Bigham, 1st Viscount Mersey

Not wanting to be outdone by the Yanks and have their own people look bad, the British decided to conduct their own hearings on the Titanic disaster. The Lord Chancellor of the British government appointed John Bigham, 1st Viscount Mersey, usually referred to as "Lord Mersey," to head the inquiry. The hearings took place from May 2 to July 3, 1912 at the London Scottish Drill Hall in London, England.

Like the American proceedings, the British hearings were heavily covered by the press, but they allowed more of the public to watch in person.

This was before television and even radio, so the public either had to see the event for themselves read about it in the newspapers.

Lord Mersey oversaw the testimonies of 100 people associated with the Titanic, many of whom testified at the American hearings, including Harold Bride, Charles Lightoller, and Arthur Rostron. Cosmo Duff-Gordon and his wife were the only survivor paying passengers who testified.

The captain of the Californian, Stanley Lord, was painted as one of the disaster's primary villains, much as he was by the Americans. He testified that his ship was unable to traverse the ice field safely in time to rescue the Titanic's passengers, which is now seen as truthful, but many of his crew contradicted his testimony.

It was also during the British hearing when the Cosmo Duff-Gordon and his wife were first accused of misconduct. In particular, the Duff-Gordons were accused of ordering their lifeboat to leave early and refused to pick up any survivors in the water.

In the end, perhaps owing to cultural differences, the British report was viewed as more measured and technical than the "in your face" American report. The British inquiry led to many of the same safety recommendations that came out of the American hearings.

Interestingly, the British hearing for the most part absolved Captain Smith and White Star Line officials of personal responsibility and blamed the disaster on accepted maritime safety practices of the time.

Belfast Cried

Although the Titanic disaster happened long before the Internet and even before television and radio, news of it spread quickly around the world. From New York to London and from St. Petersburg to Buenos Aries, the people of the world mourned for the Titanic and her passengers.

But nowhere was the mourning more pronounced than in the Titanic's home, Belfast.

When the news of the Titanic disaster reached the workers in the Belfast Harbour, it was said that all worked ceased because the workers couldn't hold back their tears. They spent the rest of the shift in mourning and then Harland and Wolff executives closed the shipyard for a day to allow the workers to be with their families.

For the workers and executives of Harland and Wolff, losing the Titanic was like losing a child.

The shipyard reopened the next day and the workers went back to work, but it just wasn't the same. From that day on there was an incredibly heavy dark cloud that hung over the Belfast Harbour. Of course, everyone knew what the source of the dark cloud was, but no one mentioned the name of the Titanic in the shipyard for several years.

And by then the golden age of the ocean liners was over.

The Wreck of the Titan: Or, Futility

Throughout this book we've discussed a number of similarities the Titanic and the Lusitania shared, but even eerie were the similarities the Titanic shared with a ship that never existed!

In 1898, American author Morgan Robertson had one of his stories published a novella titled *The Wreck of the Titan: OR, Futility.* The plot of the story was fairly standard and didn't garner much attention when it was published, although it did well enough to help Robertson's writing career and earned him some money. After the Titanic disaster, though, word about the novella began to circulate and people were convinced that Robertson had the gift of second sight.

The story follows the rise and fall, and rise again, of a disgraced American Navy officer named John Rowland. Rowland finds work as a deckhand on a ship, which is where the eeriness begins.

The ship Rowland was working on was the SS *Titan* and it was not only the largest ship in the world, it was believed to be unsinkable. It was 800 feet long, had three propellers, and carried 2,500 people.

The Titan was traveling at 25 knots when it struck an iceberg in the North Atlantic near Newfoundland in April.

Only thirteen of the Titan's passengers survived.

Of course, there were differences between the Titan and the Titanic. The Titan was on its third voyage in the story and it was an American flagged ship going from New York to Liverpool. Still, there is no denying the uncanny similarities between the two ships.

The similarities were so close and the demand for the story became so high that it was reissued. Robertson was accused of being a mystic and a psychic; how else could he basically predict the Titanic's demise people reasoned. For his part, Robertson was an experience mariner who served on many ships in the mid to late 1800s before he wrote *Titan.*

Robertson claimed that all similarities between the Titan and the Titanic were purely coincidental, but to this day many believe that it was an example of something greater at work.

The Financial Costs of the Titanic Disaster

We've discussed at length the human costs of the Titanic disaster. More than

1,500 people died when the ship sank and many times that number were affected over the loss of their loved ones. The disaster also took quite a toll on the psyche of people around the world. If the Titanic could sink, was anyone safe?

The Titanic was also quite a costly venture.

It cost 1.5 million British pounds to build the ship; but that was only part of the cost.

But the White Star Line executive knew that accidents do happen so they needed to insure their ship. The brokerage firm Willis Farber and Company took care of the insurance by creating a consortium of insurers who each took part of the risk. Atlantic Mutual was one of the major insurers, holding $100,000 share of responsibility. The total value of the insurance policy was $5 million.

The White Star Line received the insurance payout within thirty days of the disaster. The company used that money to at least partially cover lawsuits filed against them by some of the survivors and their families.

Today lawsuits are so common that we barely bat an eye when we hear about someone suing for something as silly as being served coffee that is too hot. It may have been a far less litigious society in 1912, but the Titanic disaster brought out a fair amount of lawyers who were willing to sue the White Star Line on behalf of survivors and victims' families.

The plaintiffs filed claims totally about $16 million for negligence. The White Star Line fought the lawsuit, arguing that there was a clause in the passengers' tickets that absolved them of all liability.

Eventually, as is the case so often today, the White Star Line settled out of court with victims and their families.

In December 1915, the White Star Line agreed to pay the victims and their families $664,000. Now you may be thinking that that sum is not bad for 1915 dollars, but it was quite small compared to what was originally requested and it had to be paid out among all of the plaintiffs.

The victims' lawyers came out all right, though.

The Demise of the White Star Line

Ocean liners in general were doomed to have a finite life span due to march of technology. By the 1950s, when air travel became quicker, safer, more efficient, and available to the public, the ocean liners were for the most part replaced by the airlines. The more far-sighted of the ocean liner executives knew that the change was coming and modified their companies accordingly.

The Cunard Line transitioned to become a luxury vacation company that operates hotels and cruise liners.

But the Cunard Line wasn't saddled with the Titanic disaster.

After the White Star Line executives collected their insurance and paid the survivors, they had the herculean task in front of them of rehabilitating their reputation. A good share of the public blamed the company and it didn't exactly handle things well on a public relations level. The company continued to do well, though, until World War I.

During World War I, most of the White Star Line's fleet was requisitioned by the British Navy, as were the fleets of most other British ocean liner companies. The Titanic's sister ships, Olympic and Britannic, were both used in the war, with the Britannic being sunk by a German U-boat in 1916.

The war may have hurt the White Star Line, but it was the Great Depression that proved to be the final nail in its coffin. When sales drastically decreased, the executives of the White Star Line made a bold move by merging their company with the Cunard Line in 1934 to make the Cunard-White Star Line. The company continued to use the White Star name until 1949 when Cunard bought out White Star, leaving the company as the Cunard Line with the White Star line no longer existing.

Although the Cunard Line continued as the premier ocean liner company, it was eventually bought out by the Carnival Corporation.

Tourists in tacky clothes replaced the well-dressed passengers on the high seas. The era of ocean line travel was gone forever.

Titanic Sized Conspiracy Theories

When a tragedy as big as the Titanic happens, you know there are bound to be just conspiracies just as big to go along with it. Maybe people develop conspiracy theories as a sort of coping mechanism for deal with loss.

Or maybe some conspiracy theories are true?

Whatever the case, some pretty colorful conspiracy theories about the Titanic and its demise began circulating in the days, months, and years after it sank. We've already discussed the strange case of Morgan Robertson, let's take a look at a few more of these cases.

The early twentieth century was a culturally different world than ours today. People freely mixed mysticism and other esoteric ideas with new scientific thoughts, inventions, and ideas. A perfect example of this is what was at the time the new study of Egyptology. Scholars were making great strides in the study in the early twentieth century, bringing to light new knowledge of the formerly lost civilization. While scholars were working assiduously in libraries and excavation sites, mystics in London, New York, and Berlin were claiming to be in contact with pharaohs who had been dead for more than two millennia.

William T. Stead was one of these mystics. He was quite open about his mystical beliefs concerning ancient Egypt while he was on the Titanic. Molly Brown, who had just returned from Egypt with several artifacts, was impressed with Stead's ideas and spent some time conversing with him.

A theory began circulating that the Titanic was cursed due to either Stead's involvement with ancient forces, or Brown's disturbing of an ancient tomb. The theory gained more traction after Howard Carter discovered King Tutankhamun's tomb in 1922. Eventually, the theory came to state that there was an actual mummy on the Titanic, which somehow caused the disaster.

Although Stead was a mystic and Brown was carrying some Egyptian artifacts for a museum in Denver, there was never a mummy on board the Titanic and the pharaohs never cursed the ship.

One particularly silly conspiracy theory is that robber baron J.P. Morgan somehow engineered the disaster to kill off all his robber baron competitors on the Titanic. Proponents of this theory never say how much Morgan paid the Iceberg to cooperate!

Perhaps the strangest of the Titanic conspiracy theories is that the Titanic never actually sank.

According to this theory, the Titanic was really the Olympic and that the markings on the ships were switched out after the Olympic's accident in September 1911. Advocates of the theory claim that the switch was done because the repairs on the Olympic were too costly, so the White Star Line people made the switch in order to collect the insurance money.

The victims were collateral damage.

Some versions of this theory hold that the Titanic-Olympic was already sinking when it left Southampton, while others state that hitting the Iceberg was intentional. Either way, the theories don't take into account the fact that Titanic's insurance wasn't enough to cover the Olympic's loss.

Titanic Sized Legends

Similar to the conspiracy theories, several legends, most of which were untrue, were spawned about the Titanic in the weeks and months following the disaster. We've already mentioned a couple and put them to rest – that the Titanic wireless operators were the first people to issue an SOS and that there was a Newfoundland dog recusing survivors – but there are a couple others worth mentioning.

One legend holds that in addition to the Titanic and the Carpathia, there was a third, ghost ship in the vicinity, the seal hunting Norwegian schooner *Samson*. According to the legend and one of the Samson's crew members, the Samson was illegally hunting seals in Newfoundland waters when it happened to come across the sinking Titanic. Not wanting to be caught for their nefarious deeds, the crew decided to sail to Iceland instead of helping the Titanic's survivors.

The problem with the legend is that the Titanic was in international waters, Titanic survivors never reported seeing a schooner, and the crew of the California also never saw a small ship in the area.

Another legend that was widely circulated but later dispelled involved the Titanic's builder's staunchly anti-Catholic attitudes. It was rumored that the number 390904 was printed on the Titanic, which when viewed as a mirror image appears to say "NO POPE."

The reality is that although was we saw earlier, Harland and Wolff hired almost exclusively Protestant workers, there is no evidence that this was ever done. The Titanic's actual yard number was 401 and it was never painted on the ship.

But even with the Internet, these legends continue to circulate because they make for interesting conversation and stories.

The Rediscovery of the Titanic

Today, the Titanic rests about 12,500 feet on the floor of the Atlantic Ocean in two pieces about 350 miles southeast from the coast of Newfoundland. Almost immediately after the disaster, the families of the wealthiest passengers raised money to assemble a recovery team.

But the technology of the early twentieth century made the operation impossible.

In fact, no one knew the exact location of the Titan so that by the time diving and submarine technology had advanced enough by the mid-twentieth century to allow explorers to go that deep, it was an extremely difficult and for the most part pointless venture.

None of this stopped mariners, explorers, entrepreneurs, and a few crack pots from forwarding schemes whereby they would "raise the Titanic." One person proposed using balloons, while another ping-pong balls, but they were all deemed scientifically unfeasible. Still, there were enough legitimate scientists involved in the in finding the Titanic and science had progressed far enough that the general area of the wreck could be mapped out.

The mapping paved the way for American scientist Robert Ballard and French scientist Jean-Louis Michel to discover Titanic in 1985. After the initial discovery, several expeditions followed where the wreck was documented, photographed, and many of the artifacts now in museums and auction houses around the world were brought to the surface.

Study of the Titanic has revealed that is has essentially become a new ecosystem and is extremely fragile, making any attempt to bring it to the surface highly unlikely.

Ballard and many of the scientists who've worked on rediscovering and recovering the Titanic want it to stay where it is, along with any artifacts that may still be with it. The Titanic wreck is now protected under international law by UNESCO, although that has not stopped tourists and freelance treasure hunters from visiting the site.

eBay and the Titanic

In the 100 plus years since the Titanic disaster, many of its artifacts, and more than a few fakes, have been sold in various places throughout the world. Many of the items were acquired before there was any control over the wreck, but in 1992 the rights to the wreck and the artifacts were given to RMS Titanic Inc. The company acquired 5,500 Titanic artifacts and soon began displaying them in exhibitions.

RMS Titanic Inc. was bought out by different investors and became Premier Exhibitions Inc. in 2004.

Although Premier Exhibitions owned the rights to the Titanic wreck site and possessed most of the Titanic artifacts in the world, it didn't own all of them, nor did it have any type of control over those it didn't possess. Various items continued to be sold in auction houses and back alleys, but when James Cameron's *Titanic* came out in 1997, it created a frenzy of Titanic buying activity.

1997 was also about the same time the Internet was becoming more popular and available throughout the world.

The Internet soon became inundated with people claiming to have authentic Titanic artifacts for sale. You may have seen some of these websites if you were around back then. If you weren't, then try to image the Internet as a much smaller place then it is today, much much smaller, with basically no rules. It was truly like the Wild West.

And plenty of people were falling for scams. After all, you aren't allowed to lie on the Internet, right?

By the late 1990s and early 2000s, as the general public became much more tech and Internet savvy, the Titanic scam websites began disappearing.

But legitimate Titanic artifacts continued to sell.

A violin used in one of the bands sold for $1.4 million in a 2013 auction and two menus sold for $140,000 in 2012.

And in 2017 a single cracker from the ship sold for $23,000!

If you're interested in buying something smaller and cheaper, you can find wooden splinters for sale on the Internet auction site eBay for around $100.

But what about those 5,500 items owned by Premier Exhibitions? The company went bankrupt in 2016 and put the items up for auction in late 2018 in the United States. The total value of the items have been appraised at $200 million with the minimum bid of around $20 set by the bankruptcy court. A consortium of British museums pooled their resources to make a bid, but was unable to meet the minimum requirement by October 11, 2018.

A decision regarding the outcome of the auction is yet to be rule on by a U.S. district court judge.

Remembering the Titanic

At this point you know a lot more about the Titanic then you did before reading this book and much more than the average person. With that said, as we discussed in the beginning, nearly everyone knows something about the Titanic, at least that it was a ship that sank.

Sometime, somewhere.

The reason for the public's general knowledge about the Titanic is because the disaster has been memorialized in numerous fictional accounts as well as monuments and museums.

We'll get to the fictional accounts later, but first let's take a look at some of those monuments and museums.

Statues, cenotaphs, and obelisks were erected throughout the world in places associated with the Titanic. Belfast, Southampton, Halifax, Nova Scotia, and New York are home to the majority of the monuments, but several can be found throughout the United Kingdom and the United States. Some of these are group monuments—such as a memorial to the thirty-six engineers who perished on the Titanic, which is located at the Scottish Opera in Glasgow—while others are to individuals.

A statue was even erected for Captain Smith in Lichfield, England, a city for which he had no personal connection.

There are also a number of Titanic themed museums around the world. The largest and most historically accurate is the *Titanic* Belfast, which is located in Belfast Harbour where the Titanic was built.

Although it may seem a bit tacky and tasteless, there are also Titanic museums in Las Vegas and the American tourist destinations of Branson, Missouri and Pigeon Forge, Tennessee. In reality, though, all three of these exhibitions depict the Titanic and the sinking in an accurate way that is respectful of the victims and survivors.

Fictional Depictions of the Titanic

You have probably seen the 1997 film *Titanic*, or least know about it, but there were several films, miniseries, plays, and books before that film and there have been a fair amount since. The Titanic disaster has also been the subject of episodes of television shows.

In 1912, three fictional silent films were made about the Titanic disaster, one starring survivor Dorothy Gibson, but after those there was a break in the subject matter until the 1930s. It wasn't that people weren't interested in the Titanic, but it was more so a matter of people thinking it wasn't in good taste to make such a film.

As we might say today, "it was too soon."

One of the most interesting early fictional depictions of the Titanic disaster was the 1943 German film *Titanic*. If you know if a little bit about history, especially if you've read my quiz books about World War II, then you know that Germany was under Nazi control in 1943. The film was a pure propaganda piece, portraying the British and Americans as greedy, lazy, and dumb, while the ship's fictional German first officer was sharp and able. In an ironic and tragic post-script, the ship that stood in for the Titanic, the *SS Cap Arcona*, was bombed by the British toward the end of the war, killing more than 2,000 people.

The Titanic has also been the subject of a number of television show episodes with some of the most memorable being science fiction. The Titanic featured in a 1966 episode of *The Time Tunnel*, a 1971 episode of *The Night Gallery*, and a 1983 episode of *Voyagers!*. The theme among these episodes usually involved the protagonists trying to stop the disaster, but to no avail, or attempting to help a specific individual survive.

The Titanic disaster has also been the subject of fictional books and short stories, including the 1993 book *Young Indian Jones and the Titanic Adventure* by Les Martin.

There is little doubt that the Titanic disaster will continue to inspire film, television, and book writers to include it in new stories. I wouldn't be surprised if we see a movie at some point that has zombies on the Titanic!

The 100ᵗʰ Anniversary

The 100th Anniversary of the Titanic disaster was commemorated in a number of different locations, primarily in the United Kingdom and Canada. A single flare was fired over Belfast Harbour on March 31, 2011, exactly 100 years after the Titanic came down the slipway. In Southampton, the SeaCity Museum opened on April 10, 2012, and on April 15, 2012 the cruise ship *Balmoral* made a stop at the point where the Titanic now rests.

James Cameron and Kate Winslet were also involved in media events to promote the rerelease of *Titanic* in 3D to commemorate the 100th anniversary of the disaster.

There was also an outdoor carnival in Liverpool, England to commemorate the 100th anniversary that had one strange detail. The event, titled "Sea Odyssey: Giant Spectacular," was centered around a letter a ten-year-old girl, May McMurray, sent to her father who worked on the Titanic. The girl's father perished in the disaster and the letter was return, but over the next 100 years the it acquired an almost mystical spirit to some people.

The festival featured three giant marionettes—a thirty foot tall girl, a fifty foot tall scuba diver, and a giant dog—which were led down the street by men moving cranes.

Needless to say, it was quite the spectacle, but not everyone thought it was an appropriate way to commemorate the 100th anniversary of the Titanic disaster. And if you think about it, they may have a point. After all, marionettes can be a little creepy and the image of a thirty-foot tall girl marionette is a bit off-putting to say the least.

In addition to these events, there were numerous documentaries produced about the Titanic and official postal stamps were issued by the British and Canadian governments.

Perhaps owing to geography, the 100th anniversary of the Titanic disaster was not a big deal in most of the United States.

Titanic II

The filthy rich of the world have the money to do the things most of us can only dream of. For instance, Sir Richard Branson used his money to build a spaceship and American tycoon Donald Trump used his to fund his presidential campaign. Many of the things rich people do with their money may seem trivial or even waste full to most of us, but the extremely wealthy just look at things differently.

Take the Titanic for instance.

Most of us are fine just learning about it in books and museums. But Australian tycoon Clive Palmer wants to recreate the Titanic by building an exact replica.

Well, he wants to recreate every expect for the disaster that is.

In terms of tycoons, Palmer is technically at the lower end, as he is worth $600 million, which means he isn't even a billionaire. Perhaps feeling some inadequacy in that department around his richer peers at the pollo club, Palmer announced in April 2012, just after the 100th anniversary of the disaster, that the *Titanic II*, which would be a near replica of the original Titanic, would be the flagship of his new luxury cruise company, the Blue Star Line.

The proposed Titanic II is to be slightly larger than the original Titanic is terms of tonnage and new safety features will be added and of course new technology will be used, but it is supposed to look just like the original ship.

It is supposed to. . . .

Construction was originally supposed to begin in 2012 and completed by 2016, but financial difficulties, among other things, have set the project back. The Blue Star Line announced in late 2018 that work was finally underway on the ship.

But many remain skeptical that it will ever be built.

And many are fine if it is never built, stating that they think the Titanic II is in bad taste.

With all of the setbacks the Titanic II has faced, one wonders if the ghosts of the original Titanic and the victims have conspired to put an end to the project. There are plenty of people around the world who think so.

How Do We Study the Titanic?

Hopefully you've learned quite a bit about the Titanic from this book and had at least a little fun in the process. The first thing you should've learned about the Titanic is that there was a lot more to the ship than its sinking. Really, the Titanic was the culmination of over 100 years of advances in technology.

It couldn't have happened without the success of Robert Fulton and the hundreds of steamships that made trips across the world's oceans before the Titanic.

The Titanic also couldn't have been possible with the idea and funding from the men in the front offices at Harland and Wolff and the White Star Line, but also, and some would say more importantly, the men who physically constructed the Titanic. The Titanic was truly a modern marvel, which made its tragedy that much worse.

Hopefully you'll remember the heroes and heroines of the disaster and how the Titanic has been remembered, both by scholars and in pop culture.

And perhaps that is what separates learning about the Titanic from learning about other events in history. The Titanic has become so much a part of pop culture that it is impossible to separate Titanic fact from Titanic fiction. But now that you've read this book, you can do that to some extent.

Although this book has covered all of the main points about the life of the Titanic, there are plenty of good books available if you'd like to know more. Just remember to keep an open mind and have fun while you study the Titanic!

Random Facts

1. The Titanic museums in Branson, Missouri and Pigeon Forge, Tennessee have replicas of the front half of the ship. Both museums are owned by John Joslyn, who led a 1987 expedition to the location of the Titanic wreck.
2. Although the majority of the British press took a negative view toward Senator Smith and the American investigation of the Titanic disaster, the attitude was not unanimous. The *Review of Reviews*, which was founded by William T. Stead, portrayed Smith as somewhat of a bumpkin in their coverage of the investigation, but much more honest than his British counterparts.
3. It was once thought that since the Titanic was in such deep, cold water that it would be preserved indefinitely. When the wreck was discovered, scientists were surprised to find that it was supporting a thriving aquatic ecosystem.
4. Due to the extensive biological activity on and around the Titanic's wreck, scientists believe that by 2037 there will be nothing left of it.
5. Harland and Wolff never claimed the Titanic was unsinkable, but the White Star Line claimed that in reference to the Olympic and Titanic that they were "designed to be unsinkable". After the disaster, the claim was exaggerated by the public and became part of the Titanic's mystique.
6. In the late 1800s, William T. Stead wrote two short stories about sinking ships.
7. Before Clive Palmer embarked on the Titanic II project, South African businessman Sarel Gaus planned to build a replica of the Titanic, but abandoned the project in 2006.
8. Morgan Robertson was actually very well acquainted with the sea. His father was a captain on Great Lakes ships and he began sailing as a cabin boy. He began writing sea stories when he was in his early forties, but only lived to the age of fifty-three.
9. German writer Gerhard Hauptmann penned a series of short stories that were published as a novel titled *Atlantis*. The novel

was released in March 1912 and featured ship that hit an iceberg in the North Atlanic.

10.   The British inquiry into the Titanic disaster was the longest and one of the most expensive court inquiries in British history up until that time. When adjusted for today's prices, it cost nearly $2 million.

11.   Although you can find pieces of wood from the Titanic on eBay that have been authenticated, most of the Titanic related items on that site are replicas.

12.   When the White Star Line and Cunard Line merged, they were both seeking subsidies from the British government. The government agreed to give them only if they merged and since Cunard contributed more ships in the merger the new company essentially ended the White Star Line.

13.   In 2001, and American couple were married on board a submersible that was set down on the bow of the sunken Titanic.

14. Since the Titanic disaster, about 150 people have visited the deep sea wreck.

15. Bruce Ismay testified at both the American and British inquiries into the Titanic disaster. Although neither inquiry found him to be responsible, he is remembered as one of the Titanic's primary villains. The press was certainly negative toward Ismay after the disaster, but the negative portrayals of him really began with the 1943 German film, *Titanic*.

16.   As an example of how slow news traveled at the time, when American President William Taft learned of the Titanic disaster there were few details and he was led to believe that nearly everyone survived, so he went to the theater. When he learned the truth about the extent of the disaster he immediately sent a telegram to the White Star Line inquiring about Archibald Butt.

17.   The 1958 British film, *A Night to Remember*, is considered by many to be the most accurate fictional portrayal of the Titanic disaster.

18.   Senator Smith was reelected to the Senate in 1912, although in the era long before exit polling it is difficult to say

how much, if any, influence his involvement in the Titanic inquiry had on the election.

19.   Lord Mersey already had a long career in British law under his belt when he headed the British inquiry into the Titanic disaster. He was seventy-two at the time, but lived another seventeen years to the ripe old age of eighty-nine.

20.   Director James Cameroon was already well-acquainted with the sea before filming *Titanic*. He had to do considerable research and diving for his 1989 film *The Abyss* and later went to the bottom of the Marian Trench in a submersible in 2012.

Test Yourself – Questions and Answers

1. Who is the Australian tycoon who plans to build an almost exact replica of the Titanic?
    a. Clive Palmer
    b. Richard Branson
    c. Donald Trump

2. When was the wreck of the Titanic discovered?
    a. 1913
    b. 1972
    c. 1985

3. The White Star Line eventually merged with and was consumed by which of its rivals?
    a. Death Star Line
    b. Blue Star Line
    c. Cunard Line

4. According to legend, what was the breed of dog that rescued survivors of the Titanic?
    a. Beagle
    b. Chihuahua
    c. Newfoundland

5. Which of these cities did *not* host major events to commemorate the 100th anniversary of the Titanic disaster?
    a. Chicago
    b. Belfast
    c. Liverpool

Answers

1. a
2. c
3. c
4. b
5. a